Queen Victoria
Goes to the Theatre

Queen Victoria Goes to the Theatre (Her Majesty's, 1838).

Queen Victoria Goes to the Theatre

GEORGE ROWELL

Paul Elek London

First published 1978 by
ELEK BOOKS LIMITED
54–58 Caledonian Road, London, NI 9RN

Copyright © 1978 by George Rowell

ISBN 0 236 40123 8

Printed in Great Britain by
Unwin Brothers Limited,
The Gresham Press, Old Woking, Surrey

Contents

Plates

7

Introduction

Successive generations have been fascinated by the life of Queen Victoria. As Great Britain's longest-reigning monarch her historical importance is unassailable, but the steadily growing interest in her has nurtured an image at once physically slight but psychologically formidable. In a lifespan of eighty-one years and a reign of sixty-three, her official and unofficial pronouncements must run into the thousands, yet of these only 'We are not amused' is universally remembered and incessantly repeated. Moreover this puritanical image has been extended from the Queen herself to the country she ruled and the age she dominated. 'Victorian' is still a term used to mean intolerant, out-of-date, killing joy. It has even distorted the general conception of Victorian arts and crafts. Thus Victorian architecture, painting, furniture, Victorian taste as a whole, have until recently been dismissed as unfortunate if prolonged aberrations between the civilized Georgian and the emancipated modern.

Of no branch of the arts is this more true than the drama. The Victorian theatre (unlike Victorian fiction and poetry) was certainly not fertile in great writers, at least until Wilde and Shaw startled and stimulated its last decade. It was, however, immensely productive of performers, using that term to cover not merely actors, of which indeed there were probably more giants than in any earlier comparable span, but singers, dancers, clowns, acrobats, designers, musicians, in a word entertainers. The Victorian theatregoer had an enormous appetite for entertainment, and few of her subjects possessed that appetite in greater measure than Queen Victoria. Because she never entered a theatre in the last forty years of her life, an understandable belief has taken root that the stage held no charm for her. The contrary is in fact true; from the age of twelve to the age of forty-two she attended the theatre (in all its manifestations including opera, ballet, and circus) just as often as her public and private duties allowed. She never failed to record these visits in her Journal in terms usually appreciative, occasionally condemning, always responsive. Even her self-imposed exile from the theatre did not preclude, in her last twenty years, an increasing delight in commanding the theatre to come to her. The familiar (but not for that reason false) picture of the theatre in the Victorian era is of a deep division between opera, which polite society approved and supported, and drama, which it deplored and rejected in favour of the circulating library. The Queen certainly led her people in placing opera on an artistic pedestal, but in her middle years she increasingly led them back to the playhouse, so that even when her patronage was suddenly withdrawn, this impetus towards self-respect continued in the theatre; while in her last years she conferred the accolade literally on two actors, Irving and Bancroft, and figuratively on their profession as a whole.

This much has been known, at least in the restricted ranks of theatre historians, for long enough; but the precise character and extent of the Queen's theatregoing has remained a subject of unsupported speculation. It is to replace this speculation with supported argument that the present study aspires. Such an aspiration would be vain without the permission graciously granted by Her Majesty The Queen to see and quote from papers in the Royal Archives at Windsor Castle, particularly Queen Victoria's Journal. I am grateful to Sir Robin Mackworth-Young, KCVO, the Assistant Keeper of The Queen's Archives, and his staff, especially Miss Jane Langton MVO, and Miss Elizabeth Cuthbert, to whom my debt for their guidance and help is incalculable.

I am grateful to Professor Michael Booth of Warwick University for making available to me his article 'Queen Victoria and the Theatre', originally published in the *University of Toronto Quarterly*. I also owe a particular debt to Dr M. Glen Wilson of Macalester College, USA, who most generously put at my disposal the material on Charles Kean he has gathered over many years, and by so doing convinced me that an account of Queen Victoria's theatregoing, drawing on her own words, could be attempted.

Since historical and literary studies are often described (and even advertise themselves) as 'definitive', it behoves me to insist that this study is by no means definitive. It does not claim to cover all aspects, still less include every detail, of the subject. What it seeks to do is to throw sufficient light on a topic hitherto illuminated only by the most fitful and reflected beams, that others may wish to bring their own resources to bear upon it.

George Rowell

1

The Magic Box

───❦───❦───❦───

It could be said that during a joyless childhood, marked by conflict and loneliness, riding and the theatre were the Princess Victoria's great delights. From her earliest years she was the subject of dispute between the successive governments of her uncles, George IV and William IV, on the one hand, and her mother, the Duchess of Kent, and the Comptroller of the Duchess's Household, Sir John Conroy, on the other. After the marriage in 1828 of her much-loved half-sister, Feodora, the Princess's acquaintance of her own age was restricted to the two Conroy girls, Jane and Victoire, whom she probably regarded as spies in their father's secret service. Her regular routine was made up of lessons and formal appearances, punctuated by the exhausting 'progresses' which her mother conceived a necessary preparation for her royal duties. Her only ally, the faithful Lehzen, who had been Feodora's governess before hers, was nonetheless a stern and demanding mentor. Something of the Princess's craving for young and congenial company emerges in the feverish tone with which she writes of such visitors as her Saxe-Coburg cousins, Augustus ('He assisted me in sealing my letters, and we both made a mess, and he burnt a cover in sealing it, dear boy, for me, which made us both laugh')[1] and, more importantly, Ernest and Albert.

As a result of her lonely upbringing the Princess had no opportunity for joining in nursery or drawing-room plays. When she was thirteen and being put through one of her mother's pet 'progresses', she stayed at Chatsworth, home of the Duke of Devonshire, where a large house-party was assembled. After dinner the grown-ups indulged in charades, and the young Princess, though not invited to join in, recorded the proceedings longingly in her Journal:

At about 10 the charade began in 3 syllables and 4 scenes. The first act was a scene out of *Bluebeard* . . . The next act was a scene of carrying offerings to Father Nile . . . The third act was a scene of *Tom Thumb* . . . The fourth act was a scene out of *Kenilworth* (which was the word) . . . They were all in regular costumes. When it was over, which was at ¼ to 12, I went to bed.[2]

Later she drew one of the scenes from this Never-Never-Land in her sketch-book.

Though she could not perform herself, the Princess could see others —famous actors, singers, and dancers—perform, particularly during the London 'season', and in this respect her upbringing was surprisingly indulgent. Her theatre visits predate the start of her Journal in 1832; years later, seeing a performance at Windsor of *Charles XII* by Planché (produced at Drury Lane in 1828), she noted affectionately: 'The first play I *ever* saw.'[3] To this lonely and suppressed child the Royal Box at the theatre certainly charmed magic casements, opening on fairy lands, and her delight and wonder are preserved, not only in her Journal but in the sketch-books which she filled during these years.

Not surprisingly for a child who began theatregoing before she was into her teens, the spoken word meant less than song and dance. The heroine of her early sketch-books was Marie Taglioni, the dancer who stood on her points and lifted ballet out of the Baroque into the Romantic era. When the Princess saw her in her historic role in *La Sylphide*, she seemed 'as if she flew in the air, so gracefully and lightly.'[4] In fact the dancer had already won her heart: 'She looked *lovely*, for she is all-ways smiling',[5] which seems to have been a novelty for the Princess. In the same programme she heard *La Cenerentola*, and noted: 'The sisters were two FRIGHTFUL creatures',[6] perhaps thinking of the Conroy girls, whose father presided over the Royal Box on this occasion. Even the dancers Thérèse and Fanny Elssler, whom she was later to admire, were clod-hoppers beside Taglioni: 'They are good dancers, but have neither grace nor lightness.'[7]

As yet ballet was scarcely an independent art, but rather an embellishment of opera. If the score did not provide a ballet, something would be found—often quite unrelated to the opera—and thrust in between the acts. The bill offered by the King's Theatre in the Haymarket during the girlhood of Queen Victoria was essentially a *divertissement*, but sometimes a *divertissement* provided by divinities. On 27 June 1833, for example, she heard Pasta in Act II of *Norma*; Paganini playing solo ('he is himself a *curiosity*'); Malibran in the last act of Rossini's *Otello*; and saw Taglioni and Fanny Elssler in *La Sylphide*. No wonder the Journal records: 'I was VERY MUCH AMUSED' (mostly perhaps because 'We came home at ½ past 1', and we were not yet fourteen).[8]

Greatly as she loved the ballet, the Princess's taste was formed chiefly by opera. In this respect she was fortunate in her generation, for the King's Theatre could offer her during its summer season an *ensemble* of the greatest singers of the early nineteenth century: Malibran, Pauline Viardot-Garcia, and Persiani amongst the ladies, Rubini, Tamburini, and Lablache (who was to mean more to her than any of them) amongst the men. But in her girlhood one singer above all others commanded her love and loyalty: Giulia Grisi. Perhaps it was her youth that bound the Princess to her: Grisi was only twenty-two when she made her London début in 1834, and the Princess heard her as Donizetti's Anna Bolena: 'She is a most beautiful singer and actress and is likewise very young and pretty.'[9] From that moment everything Grisi did was important. A week later, after *Otello*, 'she was called for, and she came on, led by Rubini. At that moment a wreath of roses with a small roll of paper inside was thrown on the stage; Rubini picked it up and placed it on her head.'[10] Studying Grisi meant studying music assiduously; thus next season when *Otello* was performed: 'The song which Desdemona sings when she first comes on in the first act . . . is not by Rossini; it is composed expressly for Grisi by Marliani.'[11] The worshipper also begins to assume the privilege of correcting her idol, for later that season in *I Puritani*:

Grisi was in perfect voice and sang and acted beautifully; but I must say that she shows her many fatigues in her face, and she is certainly much thinner than when she arrived. It is a great pity too that she now wears her front hair so much lower than she did. It is no improvement to her appearance, though (do what she may) *spoil* her face she *never* can, it is too lovely for that.[12]

The Duchess of Kent had not remained ignorant of her daughter's infatuation and offered to arrange a concert at Kensington Palace on the Monday preceding the Princess's sixteenth birthday. The evening was above all notable for the acolyte's first meeting with her goddess. 'Grisi is *quite beautiful* off the stage . . . She is very quiet, ladylike and unaffected in her manners. I spoke to her, and she answered in a very pleasing manner.'[13] Another highlight, for different reasons, was the late arrival of Malibran, and the resemblance to Princess Aurora's birthday, with Malibran as a quite unwitting Carabosse, is striking. 'Near the end of the 1st act [part] Mme Malibran arrived. She was dressed in white satin with a scarlet hat and feathers.' If her coach had been drawn by rats, Princess Victoria could not have reacted more strongly: 'She is shorter than Grisi and *not near so pretty*. Her low notes are *beautiful*, but her high notes are thick and not clear. *I* like *Grisi by far better* than her.' Altogether the evening was one of unalloyed happiness. 'It was Mamma's birthday present for me! Costa accompanied on the piano beautifully. I stayed up till 20 minutes past 1. I was MOST EXCEEDINGLY delighted.'[14]

The joys of that night put a new idea into the Princess's head. She begged to be allowed to study singing with the senior member of the *corps opératique*: Luigi Lablache, the bass-baritone. In September, when she was suffering another 'progress', she heard Grisi and Lablache amongst others sing *The Messiah* in York Cathedral. 'Alas! it will be a long time before I shall hear their two fine voices again. But time passes away quickly and April and the dear Opera will soon return. I am to learn to sing next year. Mamma promised I should; and I hope to learn of Lablache. What a delightful master he would be to learn of!'[15] The thought sustained her during a serious illness that autumn, and on 19 April 1836 the first lesson was given. They were to continue for twenty years and to prove an unqualified joy to the pupil. Lablache, who was half-Irish, half-Italian, and wholly delightful, accompanied, transposed to a more accommodating key where necessary, and sang by way of example. Almost all the music studied came from the opera-house, so that the Princess's knowledge of the operatic repertoire was greatly enlarged.

The Duchess of Kent was present at some of the early lessons and even sang duets with her daughter for the *maestro*, but a chaperone was hardly needed. Since Lablache was then forty-one, and growing steadily fatter, the Princess must have seen him in the role of a fascinating uncle from a foreign land rather than a romantic suitor. As he visited England only for the summer season at the King's Theatre, the lessons were necessarily limited, but his pupil never wavered in her loyalty. After the last lesson that summer, she wrote: 'I shall count weeks and months eagerly till next April, when he said he would be back in London, and when I shall resume my delightful lessons with him.'[16] In later entries Lablache is always referred to as 'my dear Master', and she was still studying with him two years before his death in 1858.

Opera was to forge another important link in the Princess's affections that summer. In May her cousins Ernest and Albert (encouraged by her mother's family, in opposition to the Princes of Orange whom William IV was sponsoring) paid a visit to Kensington Palace. During this stay the Princess saw two operas with them: *I Puritani* and Donizetti's *Marino Faliero*. *Puritani*, in particular, assumed enormous importance for her. 'The dear *Puritani*' and 'The *first* opera we ever heard together' recur constantly in later volumes of her Journal. Although she was not to see Prince Albert again for three years, her devotion to opera was greatly strengthened. During her winter exile from London at Claremont (near Esher in Surrey) she wrote to Uncle Leopold who was increasingly her confidant: 'You may understand that my *Operatic* and *Terpsichorean* feelings are pretty strong now that the season is returning, and I have been a very good child, not even *wishing* to come to Town until now.'[17] It is noticeable that the Princess refers to her Operatic and Terpsichorean feelings but omits any mention of dramatic stirrings. During these years her experience of playgoing was decidedly limited. She never saw the once triumphant Edmund Kean, whose career was drawing to a premature end in her first years of theatregoing, and his reputation for drunkenness and unreliability may have dissuaded her guardians from affording her that chance. The leading light of the legitimate stage after Kean was William Charles Macready, and although the young Princess saw him several times, her reactions at this period were quite uncritical. One of her earliest experiences of Shakespeare in the theatre, Macready's *King John*, made such an impression on her that this unconsidered piece remained one of her favourite Shakespearean plays for the rest of her life. By way of contrast she saw in the same bill 'the melo-drama of *The Innkeeper's Daughter*, which is very horrible but *extremely interesting*, but it would take me too much time to relate the story of it'.[18]

In view of her subsequent criticisms of Macready, her early enthusiasm for his acting suggests an unformed taste. At this age she responded to his more spontaneous style and compared him favourably with exponents of the rhetorical Kemble school. Early in 1836 at Covent Garden, she saw Charles Kemble, Mrs Siddons's youngest brother, in one of Joanna Baillie's ponderous tragedies, *The Separation*. Kemble, who was essentially a Romantic actor, was at every possible disadvantage, including his age (sixty), but the young playgoer did not spare him. 'Kemble whines so much and drawls the words in such a slow peculiar manner; his actions too (to me) are overdone and affected, and his voice is not pleasant to me; he makes terrible faces also which spoil his countenance and he looks old and does not carry himself well.' In short her choice is the younger man: '*I, for my part, like Macready by far better.*'[19]

In *The Separation* the Princess also saw in her first season an actress whose art she was never to admire unreservedly, though she came to appreciate and respect the woman. This was Helen Faucit, who later married Theodore Martin, destined to be Prince Albert's biographer, and who as Lady Martin achieved a special place in the Queen's affections. The first of many strictures on the actress sets the tone: 'Miss Faucit is plain and thin, and her voice is much against her . . . she rants and screams too much also, but as she is very young, they say she may *become* a good actress.'[20] The actress was in fact two years older than her critic.

Two days later the Princess, rather surprisingly, was taken in the company of Lehzen and Sir John Conroy to a 'minor' theatre, a remarkable foray outside the patented ring of Drury Lane, Covent Garden, and the Haymarket. The Olympic, however, was in a special category, for its directress, Madame Vestris, had earned for it a reputation and clientele noted for sophistication and breeding in an age of rapidly deteriorating audiences. To this end her leading man (soon to be her second husband) Charles James Mathews had contributed greatly, and although the play, *One Hour, or The Carnival Ball*, was a vehicle for both leading lady and partner, the Princess's eyes were all on Mathews. Her reactions are significant: 'He is quite a young man, I should say not more than five or six and twenty. His face is not good-looking, but very clever and pleasing; he has a very slight, pretty figure, with very small feet, and is very graceful and immensely active; he skips and moves about the stage in a most agile manner.' Somehow the writer seems to be comparing him with Macready, who wouldn't skip, and Charles Kemble, who couldn't. 'He is *so* natural and amusing, and never vulgar but always gentlemanlike.'[21]

Her curiosity was undoubtedly aroused. Two days later she discovered in Lady Burghersh someone who had taken part with Mathews in amateur theatricals amongst the English colony in Florence, when he was studying to be an architect. The secret of his age had to come out: 'Lady Burghersh also said that he looks younger than he is, for that he must be 3 or 4 and thirty', but the Princess's opinion of his gentility was confirmed up to the hilt. 'He then performed as a gentleman; he

1 and 2   Two favourites in
two favourites: Grisi and
Lablache in (right) *I Puritani*
(below) *Norma*.

3   Van Amburgh, King of the Beasts. 'It . . . made me wish I could do the same.'

4   Hengler's Circus at Windsor Castle, 1886. The Queen never lost her love of the Circus.

now acts quite like a gentleman, and looks so too; he is a charming performer, I think.'[22]

The first of her special loyalties to actors was forged; Vestris and Mathews were admitted to that corner of her affections already occupied by Grisi and Lablache. Though gossip could have supplied her with much to disparage their morals and financial sense, she never wavered in her admiration of their art. She was to support them again and again, wherever they played; and Mathews appeared in one of the earliest as well as one of the last of the Command Performances at Windsor.

Next year she sketched them as Dapperwit and Belinda in *The Rape of the Lock*, a piece by John Oxenford which owed little more than its title to Pope. The portraits, dated April 1837, are confident and accomplished, a marked advance on the juvenile efforts of the sketch-books. The following month the artist was eighteen, and as a royal personage officially came of age. The shadow cast over her for so long of a regency, nominally her mother's, actually Sir John Conroy's, was dispersed, but only just in time. Early in the morning of 20 June William IV died.

For the next two and a half years the greatest influence on the young Queen's life was to be her Prime Minister, William Lamb, Viscount Melbourne. This influence extended beyond public and private life to her theatrical education. Henceforward her Journal would record, not what Lablache taught or how Charles James Mathews moved, but what Lord M. said.

2

'Lord M. Said . . .'

If the Queen's coming-of-age less than a month before her accession had proved one stroke of good fortune, a second and perhaps even more beneficial was the support now afforded her by her first Prime Minister. Lord Melbourne was fifty-eight; ten years earlier he had lost his wife after as sensational and wretched a marriage as fate could deal him. A year later their only child also died. The young Queen was therefore as much a daughter-substitute to him as he a father-figure to her. He saw it as his duty to educate her for her exalted position, and she whole-heartedly accepted his tuition. In consequence the volumes of Queen Victoria's Journal from her accession to her marriage take the form to a large extent of the table-talk of Lord Melbourne.

A major change in the contents of this Journal, at least in its published version, is the almost total disappearance from its pages of opera and opera-singers. As will be seen, this did not reflect the Queen's withdrawal from the opera-house, but in so far as Lord Melbourne is the central character of this chapter of her life, opera commanded little space in the story. For Lord M. did not enjoy opera: ' "I despised music when I was young, beyond everything," said Lord M., "and everybody who liked it; I was very foolish." It was the fashion, he said, then, to dislike music and dancing, and to lounge upon the sofas . . .'[1] The only admission he was prepared to make was that opera might suit other people: "Music takes away the sameness of a tragedy,—that is to those who *like* it"; these last words Lord M. pronounced in a very marked and sly manner, and made us all laugh . . . Lord M. was a great actor himself, but hasn't acted for *many* years.'[2]

From this it is clear that Lord M. had once taken an interest in the theatre, and though the Journal records next-to-no playgoing on

Lord M.'s part, it is full of dark hints of Lord M.'s intimate knowledge of stage secrets. An early entry acknowledged: 'He was very merry about Theatres and has peculiar tastes of his own about actors.'[3] In fact these tastes seem wholly concerned with actresses. He claimed, for example, to have been backstage and seen Mrs Jordan plain, perhaps too plain: '... one day when he went behind the scenes with Mr Lewis, the author, they met her just coming off the stage in man's clothes; she had been acting Hippolyta.'[4] The character occurs in Colley Cibber's *She Would and She Would Not*, and Mr Lewis was 'Monk' Lewis, author of *The Castle Spectre*. Mention of Mrs Jordan placed both tutor and pupil in some difficulty. He prefaced his re-miniscence with 'Mrs Jordan was very good-natured ... George IV liked her',[5] but though it was more than twenty years since she died, the young Queen must have known that William IV liked Mrs Jordan even better, as her ten Fitzclarence cousins proved, despite her mother's insistence on ignoring them whenever they appeared at Court.

Lord M. gave her a rather different impression of the theatre from that conveyed by the discreet Lablache at her singing lessons. He clearly thought little of theatrical morals: ' "The first actresses," he continued, "began in Charles II's reign, and were Mrs Ness [?Nep], Mrs Marshall, and Nell Gwynn, all women of bad character ..." '[6] He also implied that defects of character might lead to limitations of talent: 'I asked if she (Nell Gwynn) was a celebrated Actress; in some characters, Lord M. replied.'[7] There was even an uncharacteristic cynicism in some of his comments on the actress and her temptations. When Malibran's sister, Pauline Viardot-Garcia, was hailed as a new discovery, Lord M. proved less than chivalrous: 'Talked of Garcia wishing to bring her mother with her, as she was so young. Lord M. said that formerly that was not allowed in the Green Room, and that they said, "If a girl can't take care of herself without her Mother, she can't do so with her." '[8] On an earlier occasion he 'spoke of actresses; of their marrying out of their sphere; of its often not answering', citing Maria Foote, later Countess of Harrington, and Elizabeth Farren, Countess of Derby, amongst others.[9]

Before the new Queen could put some of her Prime Minister's precepts to the test at the play, she had herself to undergo the test of her first appearances in her new character. In a world without illustrated newspapers, still less film and television exposure, such official occasions as a State visit to the theatre were of enormous interest to the public.

They represented one of the few opportunities for those outside Court circles to have a close view of their sovereign. The young Queen's first State visit to Drury Lane seems to have stimulated rather than frightened her, though in her excitement she omitted, when recording the event, to bring up-to-date the words of the National Anthem: 'I alone was seated in the box which was quite *on* the stage . . . The house was immensely full, quite crammed, and I was *splendidly* received, with the greatest enthusiasm and deafening cheering. When God Save the King was sung, the whole audience joined in the Chorus.'[10] Two days later she made a similar visit to Covent Garden: 'I met with the same brilliant reception, the house being *so* full that there was a great piece of work for want of room, and many people had to be *pulled* out of the Pit by their wrists and arms into the Dress Circle.'[11]

In general there seems to have been a clear and acknowledged distinction between a State visit and a private outing to the theatre, but the audience's curiosity and enthusiasm over their new monarch ignored these niceties. The following month the Queen returned to Drury Lane to see Balfe's opera, *Joan of Arc*, but by the start of the ballet, *Daughter of the Danube*, the public were not to be denied a glimpse of Albion's Queen:

Between the 2nd and 3rd acts of the Opera, people began to cheer and call out for 'The Queen' but were hushed down because they knew I wished to be incog. But at the end of the Opera the cheering and applause became general, and I was forced to peep out and curtsey, the people cheering and being very civil. I then reseated myself and thought they were satisfied, but when the curtain rose, a storm arose and calls of 'God Save the Queen' were heard. I then got up while they played 'God Save the Queen'.[12]

As late as January 1838 the audience was still loyally inquisitive, and when the Queen slipped into Drury Lane to see Charles Kean as Hamlet: 'They would recognise me between the 2nd and 3rd acts,— I was compelled to come forward, curtsey, and hear "God Save the Queen" sung. The house was amazingly crowded and they received me admirably.'[13] A month later, after seeing the same actor as Richard III, 'I but just escaped being recognised, for as the curtain was dropping and I left the box, they called out "the Queen." '[14]

Many of these early visits to the theatre occasioned serious discussions with Lord M. before and after the performance. Following her visit to *Hamlet*, the Queen observed 'it was a very hard play to understand',

and he concurred, declaring the end to be 'awkward and horrid', and quoting Charles James Fox as saying '*Hamlet* possessed more of Shakespear's faults than almost any other play of Shakespear.'[15] He then averred that *Richard III* which the Queen was to see the following week was 'a very fine play'. On this occasion his pupil seems to have had her reservations about his judgment, for 'He fell asleep for a little while in the evening, which is always a proof that he is not quite well.'[16]

When fully fit and awake, Lord M.'s views on Shakespeare's plays seem to have been orthodox if hesitant. He named *Hamlet* and *Macbeth* 'the finest';[17] *Lear* he felt to be decidedly primitive. 'I always thought him a foolish old fellow . . . It is a rough coarse play, written for those times, with exaggerated characters.' Then, noticing his pupil was still awed by Macready's performance in the part, he added: 'I'm glad you've seen it.'[18] He approved of Macready's return to a more authoritative text, declaring, 'It is *King Lear* as Shakespear wrote it, and which has not been performed so since the time of Queen Anne',[19] though he wrongly named the adapter who in the interim 'put a deal of stuff' of his own into it as Colley Cibber (responsible for the popular version of *Richard III*) instead of Nahum Tate (whose version of *Lear* Macready had discarded).

The highlight of the Queen's playgoing in the first year of her reign was undoubtedly the performances of Charles Kean at Drury Lane. Just as a couple of years earlier she had compared old Charles Kemble unfavourably with Macready, so now Macready seemed inadequate beside Kean, who was nearly twenty years younger. Macready was now managing Covent Garden, but when she saw him as Macbeth, the most she would allow was: 'Macready acted Macbeth, but I can not say I think he did it *very* well; he *died* very well.'[20] A month later Kean's Hamlet came as a revelation:

His conception of this very difficult and I may almost say incomprehensible character, is admirable; his delivery of all the fine long speeches quite beautiful; he is excessively graceful and all his actions and attitudes are good, though not at all good-looking in face.[21]

She contrived to see him twice as Richard III, striving to find some trace of the great Edmund Kean whose acting she had been denied: 'He was dressed exactly like his father, and all those who were with me, and who had seen his father, were struck with the great resemblance

21

to his father both in appearance and voice.'[22] As with his father and many actors before and after him, it was particularly in Colley Cibber's spurious line that Charles Kean impressed his new admirer:

The manner in which he gave: 'So much for Buckingham,' was truly *splendid*, and called down thunders of applause, as also many other of the scenes where he gets very much excited; he fought and died beautifully. He was uncommonly well disguised, and looked very deformed and wicked. All the other parts were very badly acted, and the three women were *quite detestable*.[23]

At this stage of her playgoing it was difficult for any actress to make a favourable impression on the Queen, although singers and dancers of her sex could readily win her approval.

Beyond Shakespeare her dramatic education under Lord Melbourne seems to have been scanty. He drew her attention to French classical tragedy, and deprecated the Romantic revolution which had over-taken the French stage, 'whereas formerly they never killed any body on the stage, and accused us of doing so'.[24] Occasionally he dropped hints on what his pupil should avoid, for example *The Beggar's Opera* which 'was very clever and had an immense run, but is coarse beyond conception',[25] and then, perhaps suspecting he was giving the work the flavour of forbidden fruit, adding: 'they have refined it down so much and scratched out so much as the times got more polished, that there was hardly anything good left'.[26]

For the dramatists of his own day Lord M. had no time. He seems especially to have resented any attempt to combine playwriting with politics. Thus Edward Bulwer, later known as Bulwer-Lytton, who at this point of his career was on the Radical wing of Melbourne's own party, aroused his contempt. During the run of *Richelieu* there was an exchange on the subject between the Prime Minister and one of the Queen's grooms-in-waiting: 'Mr Cowper came up to us, and said he had been talking to Bulwer about his Play, and that he wasn't at all satisfied with the way in which it was acted. "Pooh, pooh!" said Lord M., "the man's very unreasonable, he's got his Play through, and I dare say it ought to have been damned." '[27] A similar verdict was delivered on Serjeant Talfourd, an MP who also held an important legal appointment and was the author of the tragedy *Ion*: ' "He writes plays," he said, "and I don't think a man who writes plays is ever good for much else; and he is a great friend of Wordsworth's." '[28]

These summary dismissals of Bulwer-Lytton and Talfourd did not deter the Queen from sampling their work. *The Lady of Lyons* was Bulwer-Lytton's first success and one of the triumphs of Macready's management at Covent Garden, not least a personal triumph for the middle-aged manager, who had to play a gardener's boy impersonating the Prince of Como. The Queen visited Covent Garden on 3 March 1838 but saw only the last act; she returned three nights later for the whole piece. 'I think the play acts well, and I like it',[29] is her laconic comment in the Journal, but she was enthusiastic enough to send her congratulations to the author and actor-manager, whose republican prejudices exploded in an ill-tempered comment: 'It was curious to see a man of Bulwer's great mind evidently so much delighted by the praise and compliments of a little girl—because a Queen!'[30]

The audience felt a more tender concern for the little girl; in particular rumours of her betrothal to one or other of her continental cousins caused them much anxiety. At the line 'Foreign prince! Foreign fiddlesticks!' the house laughed and cheered, and the Queen was seen to smile good-naturedly.[31] She was less tolerant about some of the performances, in particular the Lady of Lyons herself. 'Miss Faucit quite spoilt the otherwise interesting and fine character of Pauline; she was quite *detestable* and *ranted*, screamed, and I may say ROARED to disgust every one.'[32] The following season she was still unforgiving: 'Macready acted exceedingly well . . . but Miss Faucit very disagreeably.'[33] Once again Macready found royal attentions wearisome:

I had undressed, and was preparing to put on my court suit, when an equerry came from her Majesty to desire me to go on, as the audience were calling for me. I did not know what to do—told him, and showed him that I was quite undressed, but that I would do whatever her Majesty desired. He left me, and I thought it better to put on my dress again, which I did, and receiving a second message from her Majesty, went on as Melnotte before the audience, and met with a most enthusiastic reception, her Majesty and the Lord Chamberlain joining in the applause . . . Went into the ante-room when her Majesty came out. Lord Conyngham called me to her, and she condescended to say, 'I have been very much pleased.' I bowed, and lighted her down. Glad to conclude a day that has been very wearying to me.[34]

Having to don court dress to 'light down' the Queen was tiresome enough, but donning it twice was intolerable!

One of the results of the regular royal visits to Covent Garden during what proved to be Macready's last season there was a gradual change of heart in the royal reaction to his leading lady. In the same week as the Queen found her still unacceptable as Pauline, she admired Macready's elaborate production of *The Tempest*, with 'Miss H. Faucit (who didn't rant) as Miranda,'[35] and in the following month *Richelieu* completed her conversion: 'It is highly interesting, I may say exciting, and never drags a moment; Macready as Richelieu acted beautifully, and Miss Faucit as Julie de Mortemar surprised me agreeably . . . The House was immensely full, not withstanding it was extremely cold, and I sat the whole time in my fur cloak.'[36]

These royal excursions into the contemporary drama seem to have weakened Lord M.'s hold over her theatrical education. The proprietors of Covent Garden having terminated his lease, Macready mounted as a final gesture an impressive production of *Henry V*. The Queen saw it on 15 July ('quite splendidly got up as to scenery etc.'[37]) and two days later talked over the matter with her tutor: ' "It's a spirited play," said Lord M. Too much of the Welshman, I said, "But that's thought very clever," he replied. The broken French of Catherine at the end, I thought absurd, in which Lord M. agreed.'[38] The pupil was growing up and turning teacher.

The performer who captured the Queen's imagination at this time was neither actor nor singer, but a circus artiste. Her lifelong devotion to the circus dates from at least 1833, when a visit to Astley's Amphitheatre to see Ducrow, most dashing of riders, as St George in *St George and the Dragon*, sent her hurrying to her sketch-book to record her impressions. The Drury Lane pantomime for Christmas 1838 was *Harlequin and Jack Frost*, and included amongst its 'turns' Van Amburgh's Lions. The Queen may have set out for the performance on 10 January 1839 with no great expectations, for the pantomime 'was noisy and nonsensical as usual'. But in the eleventh scene noise and nonsense were forgotten: 'The Lions repaid all.' Although no Adonis ('He is a very strong man and has an awful squint of the eyes') Van Amburgh fascinated the Queen by his mastery of the menagerie, which included lions, lionesses, tigers, cheetahs, and leopards: 'They all seem actuated by the most awful fear of him . . . he takes them by their paws, throws them down, makes them roar, and lies upon them after enraging them. It's quite beautiful to see, and makes me wish I could do the same!'[39] The notion of the Queen of England as a lady lion-tamer defies rational thought; nevertheless it suggests her growing appetite for authority. In the next few months she was to exercise it on behalf of Lord M. in the so-called 'Ladies of the Bedchamber' crisis, and against her mother and Conroy in the unhappy affair of Lady Flora Hastings.

Over a period of six weeks the Queen witnessed Van Amburgh's act seven times. On her third visit disaster threatened; part of the act was to place a lamb before the lion's nose,

which he as usual bore with indifference; when one of the Leopards, the smallest of all the animals and a sneaking little thing, came, seized the lamb and ran off with it; all the others, except the lion, and all those in the other cage making a rush to help in the slaughter; it was an awful moment and we thought all was over, when Van Amburgh rushed to the Leopard, tore the lamb unhurt from the Leopard, which he beat severely,—took the lamb in his arms,—only looked at the others, and not one moved, though in the act of devouring the lamb. It was beautiful and wonderful.[40]

On this occasion the Queen stayed behind after the performance to examine the beasts in their cages, which were brought back onstage for her inspection. She noticed Van Amburgh had 'a mild expression, a receding forehead and very peculiar eyes, which don't exactly squint but have a cast in them'. At a later performance 'He threw himself down on the ground with the Lioness over him; and then half lying down, allowed the Lioness to come *behind* him, and then pushed his head into her mouth; she also licked his hair (all the time behind him) like a dog would your face!!!'[41]

The Drury Lane management soon recognized their good fortune; when the pantomime ended, Van Amburgh and his Lions lent support to various operas, and the Queen sat impatiently through Rossini's *William Tell* and Balfe's *Maid of Artois* for 'what is to me worth *more* than *all* the rest'.[42] Her partiality became common knowledge. Macready confided morosely in his Diary: 'Heard that the Queen was going to pay a third visit to Drury Lane theatre to see the lions.'[43] The Queen, however, was unrepentant; when she patronized Covent Garden to see *The Lady of Lyons* again with *Rob Roy* she noted: 'I was much more amused at Drury Lane, though I liked *The Lady of Lyons* very much; but *those Lions* beat *Rob Roy* and everything else of that sort to the ground.'[44] Macready nursed his resentment; on 18 February he noted with grim satisfaction: 'Acted King Lear well. The Queen was present, and I pointed at her the beautiful lines: "Poor naked wretches!" Was called for, and well received.'[45]

Despite her passion for the circus and an increasingly critical interest in the drama, the Queen had by no means lost her taste for opera and ballet. Lord M.'s indifference to these delights result in their virtual exclusion during these years from the pages of *The Girlhood of Queen Victoria*, but her attendance in no way decreased. The King's Theatre management now loyally changed the name to Her Majesty's, and Her Majesty responded by honouring the theatre some thirty-six times during the season of 1838 and at least twenty-seven during 1839. It is instructive to compare the records of the two London theatres which recognized the Queen's succession by a change of name. South of the Thames the humble Coburg anticipated the event in 1833, and in November of that year the Duchess of Kent with her daughter recognized the tribute by witnessing a performance there of *Guy Mannering* and *Gustavus the Third*. But Queen Victoria never passed through its doors, and the Waterloo Road house was to see and suffer much before its rehabilitation as the Old Vic.

In the summer of 1839 his increasingly confident pupil endeavoured to persuade Lord M. to take an interest in opera. It became more and more difficult to resist her invitations, and eventually he accepted her offer of a place in the Royal Box for a performance of Rossini's *Otello*. Although he arrived 'near the end of the 3rd act', he could plead parliamentary duty, and the opera proceeded with only an occasional protest from the Prime Minister: 'When Garcia was called out, Lord M. said "That's quite unnecessary".' But *Otello* was followed by a ballet, *La Gitana*, and the elder statesman became increasingly restive: 'Taglioni danced beautifully, and was made to repeat the Russian dance; "That's too bad", said Lord M., "and rather a bore", which made us laugh very much. "I like very much to sit it through *once*", he said.' By the second act he was growling: ' "There's too much dancing, there ought to be more action", and after a little while: "This ballet ought to be condensed; I don't think it's a good one. You may depend on it", he said, looking at Taglioni, "this woman is changed since I saw her; she has lost her elasticity." '[46]

Time was indeed passing, and not only for Taglioni. Over the years Uncle Leopold had been quietly planning the marriage of his niece, Victoria, and nephew, Albert. The Queen professed herself too young for marriage, and Lord M. harboured a deep distrust of Germans; they smoked, and never washed their faces. Nevertheless the two brothers, Ernest and Albert, were invited to pay a second visit to England. On 10 October they reached Windsor. That night the Queen recorded: 'It was with some emotion that I beheld Albert—

who is beautiful.' Four months later to the day they were married at the Chapel Royal, St James's. A new act in the Queen's history opened.

3

First Person Plural

⚜━━⚜━━⚜

The Queen and her husband-to-be shared a deep love for music. Indeed a recent biographer, Elizabeth Longford, suggests that it was all they had in common: 'In almost every other way, Prince Albert was Queen Victoria's complement.'[1] She was an accomplished singer and dancer; he was the musicologist and composer, mainly of church music, including a *Te Deum*, *Jubilate*, and *Sanctus*, and a setting of 'Hark, the herald angels sing'. As a performer he was happiest at the organ, so that in 1850 the impressionable Lady Lyttleton declared: 'Nobody but the organ knows what is in him, except indeed, by the look of his eyes sometimes.'[2] Husband and wife liked nothing better than an evening's music-making together. 'After dinner played duets'; 'In the evening I sang to Albert'; 'Afterwards I sang and Albert accompanied me' are recurring entries in the Journal.

The Queen's repertoire, shaped and schooled by the greatly-loved Lablache, was primarily operatic. It was therefore natural that the royal couple's shared interest in the theatre should be based on the opera-house. Although the former King's Theatre had seen a good deal of the Queen before her marriage, it was to become her theatrical home, sometimes, it seemed, to the exclusion of other theatres, in the first decade after her marriage. Her Majesty's was never better named than in the 1840s. Inevitably her theatregoing was restricted by her royal and family responsibilities, particularly the latter. Of the six children born to the Queen in this decade Princess Alice and Princess Helena, appearing at the height of the London seasons of 1843 and 1846, were especially demanding. The gradually evolving royal routine also influenced the Queen's theatrical calendar, particularly after the choice of Balmoral as her Scottish home in 1847. Summer

28

and early autumn were spent there, late autumn and the Christmas season at Windsor, Easter usually at Osborne, and there were other short visits.

This pattern left the Royal Family in effect only five months for London theatregoing, but these months were put to considerable use. The collection of playbills and other records preserved in the Royal Archives at Windsor Castle may not provide complete statistics, but they do give a valuable indication of the frequency of the Queen's visits to the theatre. Three times in the first ten years of her marriage (in 1840, 1847, and 1849) the total approaches fifty. In 1852 it exceeded fifty. Given a maximum of five months spent in London, this suggests two to three visits a week, the record of a real devotee, particularly in view of other demands on her evenings.

These records also show how strong was the royal couple's taste for opera. In 1840 some forty-five visits included twenty-nine to the opera. Next year out of at least thirty-three visits, twenty-seven were to the opera. The highest figure for playgoing was in 1847, seventeen out of probably forty-nine evenings. This pattern was to be modified in the next decade, but the Queen and her husband always retained their love of the opera, and in this they reflected accurately the taste of the society they led. The theatre had already lost much of its hold on the upper classes before the Queen came to the throne, but as the drama surrendered its status, the opera-house gained in standing. The collapse of the Vestris-Mathews management at Covent Garden in 1841 and the withdrawal of Macready from Drury Lane in 1843 marked the end of the theatrical establishment. This was statutorily recognized by the Theatre Regulation Act of that year, abolishing the patents which had obtained in some form or other since Charles II's accession.

For the next ten years London's playhouses lacked leadership and continuity. Such new enterprises as arose grew largely unnoticed on the outskirts of the city, like Samuel Phelps's brave endeavour at Sadler's Wells. The heart of London's theatreland was Her Majesty's, often called the Italian Opera, and its managers built their programme around the London season. In addition French *opéra comique* was regularly played at the St James's, occasional opera seasons were staged at Drury Lane and the Lyceum, and in 1846 Covent Garden was remodelled as an opera-house which henceforward offered serious competition to Her Majesty's. Thus the London operagoer was embarrassed by riches, whereas the playgoer was on a decidedly low diet.

One aspect of theatregoing at this time which seems alien to modern taste was the practice of hearing part only of an opera or play. It was a procedure much abetted by the assorted nature of the bills—operas, extracts from operas, and ballet were offered at theatres as well as opera-houses—and by the availability of boxes with separate entrances affording private access. In this respect theatregoing must be seen as the nineteenth century equivalent of today's television, radio, and records, to be sampled and rejected at will. The high proportion of royal visits to see part of an evening's bill modifies in some degree the pattern of theatregoing which the statistics suggest.

State visits to the theatre were always a signal for loyal gestures. After her marriage the Queen looked expectantly for the public's welcome to her husband, and was not disappointed:

On entering the Box at Drury Lane, I took Albert's hand, and when we came forward, we were most tumultuously and enthusiastically cheered. 'God Save the Queen' was sung, and after that the performance commenced. Dearest Albert sat next to me, on my left . . . The first piece was the opera of *The Mountain Sylph* by Barnett, in 2 acts, the music of which is very pretty, Albert admired [it] very much. After this the people called for 'Rule Britannia' which was very badly sung and we were again much cheered. Then followed the Farce of *Raising the Wind*, in 2 acts, which made us laugh very much, and is very clever . . . The performance concluded with 'God Save the Queen' being again sung; to which had been added a verse about Albert. Just as we were getting up to leave, the cheering was tremendous, the people getting up and waving their hats and handkerchiefs. It was most gratifying in every way.[3]

Two days later the exercise was repeated at Covent Garden:

When I came forward with Albert in the Box, the applause was tremendous, as also when the special verse about him (in the National Anthem) was sung by Madame Vestris (not quite similar to the one sung at Drury Lane). It was most gratifying. The House was, if possible, still fuller, the whole so well managed and the Box so prettily decorated.[4]

These demonstrations of loyalty were often made in times of emergency. Four months after their marriage the Queen and her husband suffered the first of several assassination attempts, this one in Constitution Hill by a madman, Edward Oxford. Their next visit to the theatre was three days later at Her Majesty's:

It was the *Barbiere*, which had already begun, but the moment we entered the Box, the whole House rose and cheered, waving hats and handkerchiefs. Albert was called for separately and loudly cheered . . . Just before leaving the Opera, I got a note from Lord Normanby in which he says that the bullet has been found, and that it fits the pistol.[5]

Ten years later another would-be assassin, Robert Pate, attacked the Queen and her children while they were driving in Hyde Park. Nevertheless that evening:

As I was not unwell, though shaken, nervous and unable to eat, we decided to go to the Opera . . . Saw good Sir G. Gray before we went, he was greatly distressed and in tears. The feeling of *all* classes admirable—the lowest of the low being *most* indignant. The whole affair seems unconnected with anything. Going to and returning from the Opera we were most enthusiastically received, and the moment I appeared in the Opera House, the burst of enthusiasm was most hearty and affectionate. 'God Save the Queen' was sung, and both in the House and on the Stage there was cheering and waving of hats.[6]

On at least one occasion, however, a visit to the theatre led to an 'unfortunate incident' which upset the Queen far more than the substantiated assassination attempts. In 1848, during the Chartist demonstrations, she and her husband attended a performance of *Lucia di Lammermoor* at Her Majesty's:

Almost immediately after we had left the Opera, not far from the Duke of York's statue, a man ran up to the carriage on Albert's side, where the window was open, saying several times over something like 'a real murderer'. This frightened me dreadfully, on account of the Chartist troubles, and I could not get over it for some time. But the man gradually dropped back afterwards. The unpleasant experience quite filled my mind for a time.[7]

Not only was Her Majesty's Theatre appropriately named, but its alternative title, the Italian Opera, indicates the Queen's preference. Her loyalties in this direction had been early established. Her delight in *Norma*, together with her devotion to the 'dear *Puritani*' assured Bellini of first place in her affections for many years, and he was closely followed by Donizetti. The two composers commanded her approval far more completely than Mozart or even Rossini, and only in the 1850s were they rivalled by Meyerbeer. In the case of Bellini there were admittedly strong sentimental considerations. Not only was *Puritani* the first opera she saw with her future husband, but at

Her Majesty's in the 1840s it was sung by the famous quartet: Grisi, Rubini, Tamburini, and Lablache, and to two of these the Queen was strongly attached. Lablache was of course her 'dear Master', and for her Grisi combined voice, beauty, grace, and character, so that the emergence of such rivals as Persiani and Albertazze brought out her strongest protective instincts. As early as 1838 she had asserted: 'It was *Norma*; and great and perfect as Grisi *always* is in this character, I never saw her act with so much power, feeling, and grandeur, or sing so exquisitely or look so beautiful as she did last night. Albertazze was a complete failure as Adelgisa; she quite broke down in the two Duets.'[8] A year later, following a performance of *La Gazza Ladra*, she complained: 'It is quite mystifying to see how little they applaud poor Grisi, and how violently they do Persiani, who is not to be compared in *any* way to Grisi, and who is very ugly; it is very wrong.'[9] Even when the Queen's musical training told her a rival had emerged to challenge the beloved Grisi's singing, she could not praise her un-stintingly. In the young Pauline Viardot-Garcia she recognized a remarkable voice, but her looks were all against her: 'I must say I was delighted and astonished with Garcia's Desdemona . . . it went to one's heart, and those low notes would make one cry. She is an extra-ordinary creature, but is—oh! so sadly ugly.'[10]

The Royal Archives show that the Queen saw three of Bellini's operas, *Norma*, *I Puritani*, and *La Sonnambula*, some twenty times each over a period of twenty-five years. Her other favourite composer, Donizetti, was more widely represented in the repertoire, for he wrote two of her best-loved comic operas, *La Fille du Régiment* and *L'Elisir d'Amore*, as well as the tragic *Lucia di Lammermoor* and *Lucrezia Borgia*, which figure prominently in her collection of playbills. She attended the English *première* of *Lucia*, and was captivated at once. 'It is decidedly one of Donizetti's best operas; it is full of the most beautiful and touching melodies.' As always she was thrilled by a 'strong' situation: 'The most striking scene possible was when Edgardo cursed Lucia, which Rubini did in a manner to make me shiver, so natural, so fearful.' Even the despised Persiani was praised: 'Mme Persiani (as Lucia) sang *beautifully*, particularly in the last scene when she is mad', although she only 'looked *quite pretty*'.[11] Loyalty to Grisi was un-impaired.

For the modern opera-lover Italian opera in the nineteenth century is dominated by Rossini and Verdi. Neither won Queen Victoria's total support, although Rossini certainly figured large in her theatre-

5 and 6 Prince Albert as Edward III and Queen Victoria as Queen Philippa in 'The Queen's Masque', 1842. 'I danced a Quadrille . . . with some difficulty, on account of my heels.'

7 *The Merchant of Venice* at Windsor Castle, 1848. 'All this is dear Albert's own idea.'

8 *King John*, 1852. '. . . *what* a man Shakespeare was!'

going. *The Barber of Seville* provided her first recorded evening in the theatre (aged thirteen) and retained her affection for the next thirty years. On at least one occasion it supplied her with some unintended comedy:

Mario had completely lost his voice, and when he came on to try and sing, said 'e impossibile, non posso', bowed and went off the stage. Upon this Lablache made such a funny charming face that the whole audience laughed. After waiting a quarter of an hour, Corelli came and took Mario's part, which he did very fairly, though he did not know his part very well.[12]

None of Rossini's other comic operas pleased the Queen as greatly, though she often saw (and sang from) *La Gazza Ladra*. She heard Grisi sing Cenerentola, 'but it is not a part that suits her', and 'the opera itself is tiresome'.[13] She did not see *L'Italiana in Algieri* until 1847 at Covent Garden, when she found 'the story very stupid, but the music very pretty',[14] and two years later she judged *Le Comte Ory* 'a pretty opera, though the subject is strange'.[15] As for *Matilde di Shabran*, the Queen's comment speaks for itself:

It was *Matilde di Shabran*, by Rossini, in 2 acts, and which I have never seen before, and hope never to see again; for though Rubini, Persiani, Tamburini, and Lablache (who was very comic and ridiculous as Il Poeta) sang in it, and there are one to two pretty concerted pieces in it, it is a most heavy nonsensical opera. Mme Estherlen helped to make it more tiresome.[16]

Rossini's 'serious' works recur frequently in the repertoire during these years. The Queen continued to admire *Otello*, but had reservations on many of the remainder. *Tancredi* was 'full of beautiful music, but otherwise a very tiresome heavy Opera, the story being a most uninteresting and dull one'.[17] William Tell was a subject whom no nineteenth century theatregoer could avoid, and the Queen witnessed his story in at least three forms: Schiller's original German, played by the celebrated Emil Devrient at Drury Lane in 1853; an English version by Sheridan Knowles which was for some years in Macready's repertoire; and the opera. This she acknowledged to be 'Rossini's Chef d'Oeuvre' when she first saw it in 1839, and it then had the great attraction in her eyes of Lablache in the title role: 'Lablache's acting and singing as Guglielmo were very VERY fine; and he looked so well too.'[18] Even here, however, second thoughts modified her opinion, for she decided: 'It is splendidly and beautifully composed, but not an in-

33

teresting Opera.'[19] *Semiramide* she saw some years later. Although it 'was beautifully got up—very fine scenery, decorations, dresses etc.,' the occasion proved melancholy, for the adored Grisi 'sang beautifully, but is grown very large'.[20]

The Queen's knowledge of Verdi in performance was limited, since her widowhood and withdrawal from theatregoing cut her off from all his work after *Sicilian Vespers*. It would be an injustice, therefore, to assess her views from the comments she made on such early pieces as *Nino* (i.e. *Nabucco*): 'a wretched dull opera';[21] *The Two Foscari*: 'saw the 2nd and 3rd acts, which contain some pretty things';[22] and *I Masnadieri* which not even Jenny Lind and Lablache could save: 'very inferior and commonplace . . . he acted the part of Maximilian Moor, in which he looked fine, but too fat for the starved old man'.[23]

In the 1850s, however, the Queen saw two Verdi operas still strongly represented on the stage: *Rigoletto* and *Il Trovatore*. Her view of *Rigoletto* remains shrouded in mystery. She first heard it at Covent Garden in 1854, and her Journal reads simply: 'Went to the Opera where we saw *Rigoletto*',[24] a virtually unique instance of critical self-denial. Two years later an entry runs: 'To the Opera at the Lyceum, where *Rigoletto* was given. It was a very good performance.'[25] Still no comment on the work. This silence may, of course, have been un-intended, but a suggestion to the contrary is contained in her account of Tom Taylor's play, *The Fool's Revenge*:

Went to the Princess's Theatre (no longer belonging to the Keans) where we saw *The Fool's Revenge*, a dreadful play, adapted from Victor Hugo's *Le Roi S'Amuse*, and the same subject as *Rigoletto*, only altered. It is a most immoral, improper piece, but it was well acted . . . Our 3 girls went to the Opera to see the *Barbiere*.[26]

This is one of the Queen's strongest condemnations of any dramatic work on moral grounds, and suggests an explanation for her reluctance to comment on *Rigoletto*, however well performed. It is noticeable that neither she nor the Prince Consort (still less their three girls) seems to have braved exposure to *La Traviata*, although its first English production was in 1856.

Il Trovatore, on the other hand, she did see and enjoy—at least three times. On the first of these she noted with some discernment:

The story is very extraordinary, tragic, and interesting—the music is infinitely superior to anything I have heard by Verdi. There are many beautiful pieces—short bits, though unfortunately the most pathetic and important moments are constantly succeeded by *valses* and *galops*, as is always the case with the modern Italian school. The Prison scene is too long, but it is very suitably composed.[27]

Il Trovatore seems to have marked a turning-point in the Queen's opinion of Verdi, and it would be fascinating to know her impressions of *Aida*, *Otello*, and *Falstaff*, the first two full of the strongly dramatic situations she relished, the last commended by its subject matter.

Unquestionably the most intensive period of operagoing that she enjoyed was Jenny Lind's first London season in 1847. The excitement had built up well before her arrival, for the 'Swedish nightingale' had begun negotiations with Covent Garden, then under the management of the unscrupulous but irrepressible Alfred Bunn, whose shadow falls across so many pages of theatrical history at this time. His latest exploit was to persuade Michael Costa, musical director of Her Majesty's, to defect to the remodelled Covent Garden, together with all the leading singers except the veteran Lablache. In this emergency Benjamin Lumley, manager of Her Majesty's, saw Jenny Lind as his only salvation, hurried to Vienna, and persuaded her to sign a contract with him which was to cost him £2,500 in damages to Covent Garden.

The price was well worth paying. From her first appearance in *Robert le Diable* on 4 May, the British public surrendered to her, and no member of her audience was more her subject than the sovereign. The Queen and Prince Albert attended all sixteen of her performances, seeing her five times in both *Robert le Diable* and *La Sonnambula*, and three times in *La Fille du Régiment*. They cancelled or cut short other engagements to hear her; two days after her début, she sang in *Robert le Diable* again. The dinner party at Buckingham Palace that night included the Prime Minister, Lord John Russell, and Lady Russell, but

at half past 10 we broke up and went to the Opera to hear Jenny Lind, coming in just before the 'air de grace' and for that beautiful last act, in which there is that touching Chorus in the Church, with the Duet between Robert and Bertram, and that exquisite Trio between them and Alice, which gives me quite a shiver down my back and for which *alone* I would go to the Opera.[28]

A week later the Queen was committed to attend an amateur performance at the St James's in aid of charity, but no sooner was it over than she hurried round to Her Majesty's for the last act of *La Sonnambula*. On 28 May Lind, together with other principals from Her

35

Majesty's, sang at a Buckingham Palace concert. 'I spoke to her', wrote the Queen proudly, 'and praised her very much, and she was so modest and nice and looked so ladylike.' Ten days later there was another chance to hear, talk to, and praise her at Marlborough House, where the idol of London sang for Queen Adelaide. All the Queen's relations were urged to hear her. The King of the Belgians arrived and was duly delighted by *La Sonnambula*. 'Uncle was astonished, and said he had never heard anything so perfect before. There will, I fear, never be anything like her again.'[29]

This note of 'never more' enters early into the Queen's account of Jenny Lind. Within a week of Uncle Leopold's conversion, she records: 'Am in despair that I shall not hear her any more',[30] although she was to attend two more performances that season, eight next year, and six in 1849 during Lind's farewell appearances. No singer in 'her' roles could henceforward satisfy the Queen. Past loyalties were discarded, even to the once adored Grisi, who rashly attempted Norma at Covent Garden the night before Lind first sang it at Her Majesty's. The Queen attended and shook her head: 'Grisi exerted herself very much but has gone off a good deal in her acting, and her voice has become *passée*.'[31] Although the jealous and erring Norma was not a part that suited the devout and serious Swede, she could do no wrong: 'Jenny Lind's acting and singing exceeded all I have ever heard.'[32] Nor was Lind to be deposed, as Grisi had been before her. Three years after her farewell performance, the Queen heard *Robert le Diable* at Covent Garden: '... but Mlle Julienne ruined the part of Alice, which was Lind's *chef d'oeuvre*.' Touchingly, she adds: 'À propos of Lind, she has come over from America, where she has married a Mr Otto Goldschmidt, a young pianist, and she has sent me word, through Mr Anderson, that she was perfectly happy, and was going to Germany today or tomorrow.'[33] In fact the Goldschmidts were to spend much of their married life in England, and the 'nightingale' sang more than once at Windsor. When she died at Malvern in 1887 an Indian shawl given to her by the Queen was buried with her.

It is notable that, steadfast as the Queen remained to Lind in operas she could not wholly enjoy (*I Masnadieri*, *The Marriage of Figaro*), the parts that commanded her deepest devotion were Alice in *Robert le Diable*, Lucia, and Amina in *La Sonnambula*, in each case a pure and vulnerable girl, overwhelmed by evil powers, human and superhuman —producing those powerful contrasts which always thrilled her in the theatre. Lind may be said to have converted the Queen to Meyerbeer;

the appeal of *Robert le Diable* directed her to *Les Huguenots*, which became an enormous royal favourite in the 1850s, when she saw it some eighteen times, on five occasions in 1858 alone. It was the only new opera from which sketches were specially commissioned for the Royal Library at Windsor, although many plays were so recorded.

But if one Paris composer was the Queen's meat, another proved to be her poison. In 1853 Berlioz came to London to conduct *Benvenuto Cellini*, and suffered a right royal rejection:

Dined as yesterday and then went to the Opera, where we saw and heard produced one of the most unattractive and absurd operas I suppose anyone could ever have composed, *Benvenuto Cellini* by Berlioz, who conducted himself. There was not a particle of melody, merely disjointed and most confused sounds, producing a fearful noise. It could only be compared to the noise of dogs and cats! The 2 1st acts kept us in fits of laughter, owing to their extreme foolishness.[34]

The Queen's preference for Meyerbeer, particularly the Satanic element, may throw some light on her changing view of *Don Giovanni*. In general her attitude to Mozart was respectful rather than reverential. Even *The Magic Flute* had its limitations: 'The music by the immortal Mozart is so fine, but the story is too simple, trivial and rather absurd for our times',[35] while *La Clemenza di Tito* was an experience not to be repeated: 'the music very fine, but remarkably dull and heavy. We went away in the middle of the 2nd Act.'[36] The comic operas left her less than satisfied: she saw *The Barber of Seville* half a dozen times for every performance of *Figaro*, and found *Cosi Fan Tutte* 'too long, and the story rather uninteresting and absurd'.[37] But *Don Giovanni* grew on her as she grew; the young unmarried girl had her reservations: 'not the Opera to conclude with'[38] she wrote at the end of the 1839 season, but the mature woman found it endlessly fascinating. Six years later she declared: 'The more I see *Don Giovanni*, the more I admire it, the music is so splendid',[39] and it seems to have been the first opera her children witnessed. On 14 June 1851 she recorded: 'Took the 3 eldest children to see *Don Giovanni* from beginning to end, at Covent Garden Italian Opera. They were quite delighted.' On the ten-year-old Prince of Wales it may have had an even stronger influence than his parents intended.

The Queen had no opportunity of hearing Wagner in the opera-house, although his music figured in concerts at Windsor and Buckingham Palace. She did, however, see a substantial amount of English opera, including many of Balfe's works (*The Siege of La Rochelle; Joan of Arc; Keolanthe; The Bohemian Girl; The Bondman; Falstaff; The Rose of Castile; St Mark's Eve; Satanella*).There is usually a note of condescension in her assessment of these; some are 'bright' or 'pretty' but little else, and *The Bondman* was 'too long and badly sung and acted'.[40] Wallace's *Maritana* did not even measure up to Balfe: 'extremely mediocre and very badly sung', and its offence was compounded by following 'a most wonderful performance of a Professor Reilly and his 2 sons, boys of 12 and 13. Never did we see anything like it; their strength and agility and the awful things they did, seeming to have no bones at all'.[41]

When writing of English music and singers, the Queen seems to be deferring to the continental standards of her husband. There is a note of relief about his reactions in February 1843 to an old favourite of adult and juvenile theatre, *The Miller and his Men*, 'which I was very pleased to see again with Albert, who was most interested in it and admired Bishop's music very much',[42] and a distinct embarrassment when an English singer intruded on the sacred ground of Her Majesty's in *La Sonnambula*: 'Signor Borrano (son, I believe to Dr Boisragon of Cheltenham), Rodolfo. Signor Borrano is, I grieve to say (as he is an Englishman) very bad.'[43]

For the Queen whose love of the theatre may be said to have been born with the ballet, it remained a source of wonder and delight, however deeply immersed she had become in opera and drama. Inevitably time took an even heavier toll of the dancers she idolized than the singers, but there were new idols to take their places. She saw the famous *pas de quatres* danced by Taglioni, Cerito, Carlotta Grisi, and Grabu, and noted: 'Taglioni danced wonderfully and with such grace, but she is too old now to give real pleasure . . . Carlotta Grisi certainly "emportait la victoire", and is charming.'[44] Cerito was already an established favourite. Four years earlier she had appeared in a *pas de trois*:

I really never saw anything more beautiful than the way in which she danced, she literally flew, and so softly and lightly, but with such pleasing grace. She was immensely applauded, and bouquets and wreaths were showered down to her. We heard afterwards that she had particularly exerted herself as she knew I wished her to dance.[45]

As a contrast from the ethereal, sometimes morbid, tone of the

Romantic ballet, the Queen relished Fanny Elssler in the stronger measures of her famous Cachucha.

Nor was the Queen's passion for the dance limited to admiring the great ballerinas. In the early years of her marriage Buckingham Palace was the setting for a series of costume balls, in which she and Prince Albert played the leading roles. There was a 'Georgian' Ball in 1845, and a 'Restoration' Ball in 1851, but the most spectacular occasion was undoubtedly the Queen's Masque held on 12 May 1842. The royal couple appeared as Edward III and Queen Philippa, and the Queen was so enchanted by their costumes that she sketched them in water-colours in her Journal. Some of the other costumes are recorded in words:

Lord Liverpool . . . really beautifully got up in a tight white satin dress, his arms embroidered in gold all over it, red hose and gold shoes, a long mantle and a velvet cap . . . Sir C. Napier as Mahomet Ali, exactly like Wilkie's picture, was perfect, and an excellent idea. There was also a Mr and Miss Elliott in *real* Chinese dresses . . . The procession walking up slowly, 2 by 2, hand in hand, and bowing at the foot of the Throne, made a very fine effect.

The Queen does not conceal the difficulties of dancing in period costume:

After we had been to the Closet, to rearrange my crown, we went to supper, and then saw 2 Reels danced in the Ball Room, and I danced a Quadrille with George,—I own with some difficulty, on account of my heels. We did not return again to the Throne Room, and left the Rooms at a quarter to 3.

Late hours presented no problem to her, but for Prince Albert, always liable to nod off after ten, such occasions must have proved something of an ordeal.

Any comparison between the Queen's operagoing and playgoing in the 1840s suggests the difference between dedication and duty. The figures already quoted illustrate the infrequency of royal visits to the play, which may be divided into official occasions and loyalty to old favourites. Amongst the latter Madame Vestris and Charles James Mathews took pride of place. As a girl the Queen had risked comment by patronizing the Olympic, a 'minor' theatre, to see them in minor comedy. When they took over a patent theatre, Covent Garden, from Macready, she felt both a personal and an official obligation to support them. The state visit after her wedding was followed almost immediately by another to see Leigh Hunt's only play, *A Legend of Florence*. 'Mr C. Mathews received us and we talked to him. His manner is just the same off the stage as on it',[46] wrote the Queen, who was regularly surprised in her youth that comedians should be comic off the stage, just as in old age she was impressed to find them gentlemen.

Mathews sustained his reputation that evening in *He Would Be An Actor*, one of his multiple-role pieces, in which he 'was perfect as the French lady, and made us laugh immensely. Bartley [the stage-manager] accompanied us downstairs, and I told him the 1st piece was beautiful, to which he replied that it would make the author very proud.' Considering that Leigh Hunt had spent eighteen months in gaol for libelling George IV as Prince Regent, this was perhaps more tactful than truthful.

Vestris and Mathews had strengthened their company by inviting Charles Kemble (now sixty-six) back to the theatre his family had for so long controlled, and the Queen saw him as Hamlet (when 'he acted most beautifully and looked very well and quite young'),[47] Mercutio, and Benedick. She was not wholly uncritical, finding *A Midsummer Night's Dream* (with Vestris as Oberon establishing a nineteenth century tradition) 'spoilt by the introduction of stupid duets and songs',[48] though her protective scruples did not extend from Shakespeare to Milton. When she saw *Comus* she was especially struck by 'the first scene with the Procession of Comus, and the first Bacchante (Mme Vestris) seated in a car, drawn by tigers, who were remarkably well trained'.[49] A less happy occasion was *The Marriage of Figaro* (with Vestris as Cherubino) 'very badly given', and moreover 'it was melancholy to think it was the last night of Mme Vestris's management'.[50] The expense of running a patent theatre had defeated her as it had defeated more provident managers.

Infrequently as the royal couple visited the play during these years, they did see in a single week in 1841 two of the longest-lived comedies of the century during their original runs. Bulwer-Lytton's *Money* at the Haymarket was found 'very lively and clever, the plot laid in the present day. Macready acted very well'.[51] The Queen had some reservations about *London Assurance*, with which Vestris and Mathews were staving off bankruptcy at Covent Garden. 'There were some good bits in it, but if it were not for the excellent actors, I hardly think it would do well',[52] although she was to come to admire the young author, Boucicault, and his work greatly.

Macready's assumption of the management of Drury Lane—the last chapter in its patent history—predictably failed to stir in the Queen's heart the sympathy she had extended to Vestris and Mathews at Covent Garden. She saw him twice in *Gisippus*, finding it 'a beautiful and highly interesting play'[53] (which Macready did not), and once in *Macbeth*, 'which Albert had not seen before'.[54] Her highest praise was reserved for Macready's elaborate production of *Acis and Galatea*, in which his designer excelled himself: 'The scenery, painted by Stanfield, is quite superb, particularly the scene of the sea, which is the opening scene, in which the waves roll most naturally and the sea comes in and recedes, just as we so often watched it at Brighton.'[55] After that other demands kept the Queen away from Drury Lane until it was represented to her that Macready was surrendering his burden, and an official visit of recognition would be appropriate.

This gesture (some sort of forerunner to a theatrical knighthood) took place on 12 June 1843. *As You Like It* and *A Thumping Legacy* were commanded. ('I was much annoyed by the selection', recorded Macready glumly, 'which does me *no* good'.)[56] His sovereign did not agree: 'Macready acted the part of Jacques and pronounced the famous speech about the Ages beautifully.' Helen Faucit also took a step closer to royal approval: '. . . but what surprised me most of all was the really beautiful acting of Miss H. Faucit as "Rosalind". She looked pretty in male attire and was lively and "naive".' There was more confusion about calls. 'Was called for', notes Macready, 'and the Queen sent to order me to go on, but I was undressed.' Nevertheless the evening ended with congratulations all round:

When the Queen came from her box, she stopped Lord Delawarr and asked for me. She said she was much pleased and thanked me. Prince Albert asked me if this was not the original play. I told him: 'Yes, that we had restored the original text.' After lighting them out, I went into the scene-room, which was filled with people, all delighted with their evening.[57]

The change in the theatrical scene, caused by the abolition of the patents the same year, brought about a change in royal theatrical habits. With official visits to Drury Lane and Covent Garden no longer requisite, the Queen was free to indulge her taste and her husband's. One theatre increasingly commanded their patronage. The St James's was the nearest to Buckingham Palace, and had been allowed to operate without a patent by some degree of Court connivance. Aware of this privilege, the management tactfully changed its name after the royal wedding to the 'Prince's', although this was soon dropped. Another innovation about this time survived: the adoption of the St James's as a home for French plays and opera (recognized by its billing as the 'Théâtre Français, King Street à Londres'). For up to six months of each year visiting French actors played a round of their famous roles. The two giants who thus appeared were Rachel and Lemaître, but there was a steady traffic of other leading names from the Paris stage: Plessey, Rose-Chéri, Doche, Déjazet, Lafort, Bouffé. The Queen and Prince Albert took a box for the first season, 1840, and remained regular patrons of the theatre until the French visits ended in 1859.

The St James's role of 'Théâtre Français' was regarded by London society in the same light as Her Majesty's of the Italian Opera. It offered art in a more refined, more exclusive form than English performers could achieve, and royal patronage amply confirmed the privileged position of both houses. In 1847, out of forty-nine recorded royal visits to the theatre, thirty-two were to the opera, fourteen to the St James's, and of the remaining three, one was to an amateur performance, another (by Prince Albert) to the Latin play at Westminster School. Only one was to an English play by an English company, at the Haymarket.

That this preferential treatment was deliberate is clear from a comment the Queen made to her eldest daughter soon after her marriage and arrival in Berlin:

... as regards the French plays—you should go; there are many—indeed quantities of charming little plays—and dear Papa—who you know is anything but favourable to the French—used to delight in going to the French play—more than to any other, and we used for many years—when we had a good company (we have had none since 54) to go continually and enjoyed it excessively.[58]

Where the Crown led, the court followed. 'There were quantities of people one knew in the Theatre',[59] the Queen observed after a visit to the St James's in 1843. Of no other London playhouse would she be able to say this for the next ten years.

The prestige of the 'Théâtre Français à Londres' was undoubtedly established by the triumph of Elisa Félix, who acted under the name of Rachel. She first appeared in London in 1841, and so great was the interest in her, that Her Majesty's was chosen as the scene of her début, but all her subsequent appearances were at the St James's. On Rachel's first visit the Queen saw her in *Horace, Maria Stuarda,* and *Bajazet.* In the former she found the French tragedienne 'simple, natural, and unaffected',[60] a somewhat surprising reaction, but she had already heard and met the actress after a recital at Marlborough House two days earlier. She pronounced herself a convert not only to Rachel but to Racine and Corneille, which 'much as I admire them to read, must always be to a certain extent formal and stilted, but Mlle Rachel is perfect in her interpretation of the different roles. After her last Recitation, we talked to her. She is striking looking, and has a re-markably pleasing, modest manner, and is altogether a most interesting personality. She is only 19.'[61]

Four subsequent visits to London were to revise somewhat the Queen's view of French tragedy but not of Rachel. *Polyeucte* remained untainted; she saw it in 1851 with Rachel and her brother, and noted: 'All that Polyeucte, a Christian martyr, says is very fine',[62] but Rachel's greatest vehicle, *Phèdre,* left her not merely stunned but a little shocked: 'Mlle Rachel's acting was very fine, as also her brother's, M. Raphael Félix, as Hippolyte. But the French Tragedy is not pleasing, and extremely unnatural.'[63] Even *Andromaque* was bitter-sweet: 'A very fine tragedy, in which Rachel acted the abominable character of "Hermione" beautifully.'[64]

Consequently the Queen must have been grateful for the 'Théâtre Français' frugality with classical tragedy, and indeed with the classical French repertoire as a whole. No other French artiste offered her Racine or Corneille, and she saw Molière only twice: *Le Misanthrope* ('We came in for the end')[65] and *Les Fourberies de Scapin* ('Molière's admirable comedy').[66] The Romantic drama was more widely represented. Rachel duly thrilled the Queen in *Adrienne Lecouvreur*: 'It is a beautiful character, and Rachel's delineation of it is one of the finest pieces of acting imaginable—such a refinement of feeling and expression of passion, love and sorrow, and such a fearful way of depicting death—of the delirium produced by poison. I frequently felt tears in my eyes.'[67] Lemaître of course was the French Romantic actor *par excellence,* and he succeeded in reconciling royal English delicacy to such sensational pieces as *Trente Ans dans la Vie d'un Joueur* ('very interesting but dreadful . . . we only got back at half past 12')[68] and *Don César de Bazan*: 'Lemaître is no longer young, I should say past 50; he depicted quite admirably the 'aventurier' character of Don César, full of noble and generous feelings.'[69]

Lemaître was in fact forty-five, but time was running out for him, and when, seven years later, he attempted Ruy Blas, the Queen was neither noble nor generous:

We went to the French Play and were not edified by the 4 long acts of the 5 act Play of *Ruy Blas* by Victor Hugo. It is false in sentiment, and throughout devoid of all right and noble feeling; it is really of the worst tendency, placing the unfortunate Queen of Spain in the most humiliating position imaginable. Ruy Blas, the hero, was very badly acted by Lemaître, who besides being very old, without a tooth in his head, which renders him scarcely intelligible, and with a cracked voice, is devoid of all dignity. It was a disagreeable performance.[70]

This summary dismissal is in remarkable contrast with the Queen's sympathetic view of Charles Kemble playing Hamlet at sixty-six, and is a rare instance of prejudice engendered in her by what she felt was a play's *lèse-Majesté*.

The vast majority of the French plays offered her at the St James's were neither classical nor romantic, tragedy nor comedy; they were *petites pièces* by contemporary but mostly forgotten authors, pleasing but expendable. A few titles may serve to define the *genre*: *La Jeune Femme en sa Colère; L'Ange au Sixième Etage; Le Mari à la Campagne; Un Secret; La Demoiselle à Marier; La Mère de Famille; L'Heritière; La Joie Fait Peur*. The usual, if not invariable, reaction to these pieces in the Journal is 'charming'. The reaction to their performance is generally stronger; French acting was almost always pronounced more polished and elegant than its English counterpart. Thus the Queen, after seeing a performance of *La Dame de St Tropez* at the St James's, could dismiss a performance by the Haymarket Company of *London Assurance* as 'abominably acted—such a contrast to last night, when all acted so well'.[71] The same play, it seems, was a different experience when given by French and English artistes. Before his fall from grace Lemaître could charm the Queen in *Don César de Bazan*, but an entry for 4 April 1851 records a double disappointment: 'We dined alone, and Albert went to hear a Lecture of Sir Charles Lyall's on antediluvian raindrops, whilst I, with the Ladies and Gentlemen, went to the Haymarket and heard 2 acts of *Don César de Bazan*, which is not so good in English.' It may of course have been the loss of the antediluvian raindrops rather than the translation of the play which left the Queen dissatisfied.

Undoubtedly the royal preference for French plays and Italian opera in the 1840s produced a certain degree of resentment in the English theatrical profession and the English press. In 1847 the double attraction of Jenny Lind at Her Majesty's and Rachel at the St James's had drawn the court and fashionable society to these foreign shrines in unprecedented numbers and frequency. No wonder the Queen wrote on the last night of her residence at Buckingham Palace: 'This was quite the finish of our London gaieties.'[72] 1848 was a very different year—the year of revolutions in Europe and demonstrations in England. At this juncture it was unwise of the Drury Lane management to invite the Cirque Nationale de Paris to appear, and no less unwise of the Queen's advisers to encourage a visit by the royal children. The circus was followed into Drury Lane by the Théâtre Historique in a repertoire of French historical romances. Benjamin Webster, manager of the Haymarket, petitioned parliament to limit the number of foreign companies allowed to appear in London; the *Theatrical Journal* asked 'Is This The Time To Call Upon The English Nation To Support A French Company?'; and the performance of *Monte Cristo* at Drury Lane on 12 June produced what the *New Monthly Magazine* called 'The greatest theatrical uproar known in London since the days of the O.P. [the Old Price riots at Covent Garden in 1809].'[73]

In this emergency Court circles clearly advised the Queen and Prince Albert to cross the road from the Italian Opera House to the eminently English Theatre Royal, Haymarket, where Charles Kean and his wife were appearing. On 3 July they attended a Command Performance for the Keans' benefit of *Money* and *The Wonder*. A further Command was given to Macready, who was about to embark on an extended (and as it proved disastrous) American tour, involving him in the notorious Astor Place Riots. He had replaced the ill-fated Théâtre Historique at Drury Lane, and on 10 July the Queen attended a performance there of *Henry VIII*, 'which was not well acted or produced, Macready himself made but an ineffective Wolsey'.

These two Command Performances were only the first indications of a decision to place 'by Royal Appointment' firmly over the English theatre. A series of Command Performances at Windsor Castle was being simultaneously planned, and its direction offered to Charles Kean. On 13 July, only ten days after his Haymarket benefit, the actor wrote from Liverpool to his mother:

I have scarcely had time to *think*, much less to write ... I have received the most flattering acknowledgments from the Court relative to our Benefit. The Prince told Lord Morley, that the Queen and himself were delighted

45

and were much more pleased with my Don Felix, than with Charles Kemble.

I have received instructions to give English performances once a week at Windsor Castle, commencing after Christmas—for six weeks.

This is a grand business and will be of the utmost service to me—I shall probably detour one day passing through London on purpose to see Col Phipps about it at Buckingham Palace, and therefore you may expect me on Monday 24th July.[74]

The 'grand business' was under way.

4

Welcome to Windsor

The sequence of events in the summer of 1848: press and public agitation against foreign intruders in the London theatre, two Command Performances by English companies in quck succession, and the approach to Charles Kean—suggest the immediate origins of the series of Windsor Theatricals which was to extend over a period of twelve years. Undoubtedly, however, some such project had been under consideration, particularly by Prince Albert, before these events. He was bound to contrast the flourishing Court Theatre at Coburg with the total absence of such an institution in a country as rich and influential as England. In one of the letters she addressed to the King of Prussia, written from Windsor on 6 January 1849, the Queen mentions his representative at the English Court as advising her on the subject:

Chevalier Bunsen has been helping us in an attempt to revive and elevate the English drama which has greatly deteriorated through lack of support by Society. We are having a number of performances of classical plays in a small, specially constructed theatre in the castle, and are collecting what still remains of the older art. The stage has been erected in the room which you occupied, the Rubens rooms, and I never enter it without the most vivid recollection of your dear visit, already seven years ago. May it soon be repeated![1]

The choice of the Prince's private secretary, Charles Beaumont Phipps, as the intermediary between the Court and Charles Kean also underlines his initiative; in the following year Phipps became Keeper of the Privy Purse to the Queen, and in this capacity controlled the Windsor performances throughout their history. A triumphant entry

47

in the Queen's Journal after the first performance on 28 December 1848 concludes: '... Everything went so smoothly, there was not a hitch of any kind; all this is dear Albert's own idea, admirably carried out by Phipps and Charles Kean.'

The choice of Windsor (rather than Buckingham Palace or another of the royal residences in London) stresses the family appeal of these performances, whatever their wider significance. Windsor was the Royal Family's Christmas retreat, and all the performances were given during the Christmas season. A few preceded Christmas itself, but the great majority took place, as Charles Kean's letter indicates, at weekly intervals during late December and January. Over eleven seasons fifty performances were given, the highest total being six (1853–4) and the lowest two (1850). The decision to make the 1858 performances part of the celebrations of the Princess Royal's marriage to Prince Frederick William of Prussia and to stage them at Her Majesty's led to bitter controversy in the press and much jealousy in the theatrical profession, as will be seen, emphasizing the wisdom of restricting the series to Windsor and rejecting the idea of a specially built or adapted Court Theatre in the capital. On the other hand the plays performed at Windsor were without exception English, given by English players, and there was no opera or ballet. The Queen's reference in her letter to the King of Prussia to 'an attempt to revive and elevate the English drama' was by no means an empty phrase.

The Rubens Room (now known as the King's Drawing-Room) which Frederick William IV had occupied in January 1842 when he stood as godfather at the young Prince of Wales's christening, was not large, and by the time a stage 24 feet wide by 34 feet deep had been erected,[2] the space left for the audience must have been severely limited. The company too suffered from lack of space. The actors dressed in the King's State Bedchamber, which led out of the Rubens Room, the sexes being suitably segregated by a 7 foot canvas partition in blue and white.[3] The Queen noted: 'Half of our private band was stationed in the next room to our right; they played an Overture and also between the acts.'[4] At the same time she is at pains to emphasize the advantages of a small auditorium, no doubt contrasting it with such cavernous halls as Drury Lane and Covent Garden. 'The beauties of the language were heard and understood as they hardly can be in a large theatre', she wrote after the first play, *The Merchant of Venice*, and of *Hamlet*: 'The whole play was so impressive, from not a word being lost.'[5] Notwithstanding the limited space, the scenery and staging

9 The Emperor and Empress of the French with Queen Victoria and Prince Albert at Covent Garden, 1855. '. . . making it as clear as I could that *he* was the principal person on this occasion.'

10   *The Corsican Brothers*, 1852.
The blood-stain on Louis dei Franchi's shirt is in red.

11   *The Colleen Bawn*, 1861.
The Queen's last visit to the theatre.

were evidently elaborate. Thomas Grieve, a distinguished scene-painter from a family of distinguished scene-painters, was commissioned to supervise arrangements for the first season, and submitted the following account:[6]

Timber for Stage and Framework to suspend Scenery	£ 50	14	0
Labour in constructing the above	£ 75	0	0
Nails, Screws, etc.	£ 5	0	0
Frames and Canvas for Proscenium and Stage Doors	£ 15	0	0
Decorating the above	£ 25	0	0
Painting and Designing 8 Scenes (as per list)	£120	0	0
Rollers, Battens, Canvas, Rope and Pulleys for the above	£ 50	0	0
Painting 16 Wings	£ 20	0	0
Canvas and Frames for Do.	£ 16	0	0
	£376	14	0

Subsequent entries in the Journal regularly stress the skilful staging: *The Tempest* in 1854 was 'really beautiful and quite wonderful for so small a stage',[7] and in *Macbeth* the previous year: 'The scenery, including the Cave or Cauldron scene, with the apparitions, was admirably managed, and the dresses beautiful and most correct.'[8]

Nevertheless the limitations of the Rubens Room became increasingly apparent, and following a break in 1854–5 a move was made to the adjacent St George's Hall. This immensely long, high, and narrow room, however impressive, scarcely suggests a theatrical auditorium. Audibility was evidently a problem. Following the first performance there (*The Rivals* on 21 November 1855) the Queen noted: 'There was a performance in St George's Hall, which was divided in 2, and a stage erected with an Orchestra in front. It really looked very pretty, but we were rather too far off, and some did not hear well, but this can be rectified.' After Christmas a double-bill (*The Wonderful Woman* and *Only a Halfpenny*) justified the Queen's confidence: 'All the objections put forward last time to a theatrical performance in St George's Hall were overcome, and nothing could have been better or prettier than it was.'[9] Nevertheless comedy and farce must have seemed decidedly dwarfed in these surroundings. The most suitable choice for performance in a panelled hall, decorated with royal portraits through the ages and the arms of all the Knights of the Garter since 1348, was certainly *Richard II*, which Kean played there on 5 February 1857. Even though he was 'labouring under a bad cold and gout!', the Queen decided he 'was never seen to greater advantage', adding: 'It was curious that a Play, in which all my ancestors figured, should just have been performed in St George's Hall.'

From the start the royal children appear prominently in their mother's accounts of the series, although the Prince of Wales missed the very first performance, owing to an unfortunate accident that morning: 'He and Affie hung on an iron gate down in the Slopes which Affie pulled open, and which was off its hinge and fell; in falling Bertie got caught in it, and it fell with all its weight on his poor nose. It might have broken his nose, but thank God only broke the skin.'[10] He was, however, able to join Affie (Prince Alfred, Duke of Edinburgh) and the Princess Royal for *Used Up* and *Box and Cox* a week later. It is presumably of Affie whom Fred Belton, an actor in Kean's Company, is thinking when describing thirty years after the event the performance of *Henry IV: Part I* in 1852:

Prince Patrick (if my memory serves me rightly) had been permitted to view a portion of the performance, being then too young to remain the entire evening. At a given period between the acts a servant stepped forward; the young Prince, understanding the signal, rose without any apparent regret, though doubtless he suffered from the privation. He turned gracefully to his Royal mother, who extended her hand, which he kissed reverently, then turning to his father, who stooped as if to whisper some direction, but I saw a loving kiss imprinted upon the boy's cheek. The young Prince, bowing to the guests, went his way, without looking back, out of the door, and disappeared most charmingly.[11]

As the series progressed, as many as six royal children were included in the audience. Originally they sat on the steps of the royal dais, but by 1853 the Queen noted: 'Vicky sat with us on the "estrada", being too tall to sit lower! How time flies!'[12] At the performance of *Henry IV: Part I* the Princess Royal was much embarrassed by her brother's conduct. Fred Belton describes how, during one of Falstaff's soliloquies:

The Royal heir to the throne of England became so engrossed with the comicality of the scene (admirably played by Bartley) that he was carried away completely. He wore a tartan dress, and as tears of laughter rolled down his cheeks in his ecstasy, he rolled up his tartan and at the same time rubbed his knees with great gusto. His sister, the Princess Royal, saw with horror the innocent impropriety, and never shall I forget her terrified glance round the room. However, finding that all were intent upon the scene, she gave one vigorous tug at the tartan, which restored propriety and brought the happy boy to a sense of the situation.[13]

Of the younger children, Prince Arthur seems particularly to have cherished the performances. He first attended at the age of five, and the Queen notes he 'was very important, insisting on having a card of invitation, and then feared they would not know where he lived'.[14] For *The School for Scandal* a year later: 'Lenchen [Princess Helena] remained quite to the end, but Louise and Arthur went away after the 3rd Act. I never saw a child pay such attention, or take such interest in everything as the dear little fellow.'[15] The Duchess of Kent regularly came over from Frogmore to join the audience. After *Henry IV: Part II* in 1853 Charles Kean wrote to his niece, Patty Chapman: 'The Duchess of Kent exhibited her admiration of the last two acts by going fast asleep on the Royal dais.'[16]

The choice of Kean as Director of the Windsor Theatricals (in effect, if not in name, a resuscitation of the historic office of Master of the Revels) caused a certain amount of surprise and a good deal of jealousy. In 1848 he was thirty-seven, had yet to run a theatre, and had spent much of his career playing in the provinces and America. Macready and Charles James Mathews were considerably older and were both experienced managers. But Macready, besides being constitutionally quarrelsome, was committed to an American tour, while Mathews was notoriously improvident. Kean had nothing against him, and two major assets in his favour: his famous father and his greatly talented wife, the former Ellen Tree, who was better known (and a better Shakespearean performer) than he. The invitation to Kean in fact proved a wise and successful decision. He retained overall responsibility for all the performances until 1857, and either he or Mrs Kean (usually both) appeared in twenty out of the thirty-six given during these years.

The difficulties of assembling casts and preparing the performances cannot be overestimated. Inevitably Kean called on existing companies (his own, when he took over the Princess's, the Haymarket under Buckstone, Mathews and his Lyceum colleagues). Even so, there were always gaps to fill. Kean did not flinch from strengthening the cast from the ranks of his rivals, notably by inviting Samuel Phelps to join him in *King John* (as Hubert de Burgh) and *Henry IV* (as the king), and to play Henry V. Relations with his fellow-managers were predictably strained: Charles James Mathews regularly sulked, especially when Kean vetoed the suggestion that he double Sir Fretful Plagiary and Mr Puff in *The Critic*.[17] The one occasion on which Macready appeared at Windsor was even more fraught. He agreed to play Brutus to Kean's Antony in *Julius Caesar*, but an inevitably tense situation was greatly aggravated by the dangerous illness of his eldest daughter. Under this pressure he declined to correspond with Kean except through his solicitor, appealed (successfully) over Kean's head to Phipps regarding the casting of Lucius, and travelled to Windsor by private train.

The ensuing combat resulted in the Queen's view in a knock-out victory for Kean:

Kean's acting was quite perfection, and he gave the celebrated speech in the Forum admirably. Poor Macready I thought not good, ranting too much and being so affected in manner, and his voice cracking and puffing and having an unpleasant way of stopping between every word. The quarrelling scene with Cassius was the only one in which he acted well.[18]

Kean's Windsor triumph in *Julius Caesar* was particularly timely. He had decided to take a lease of the hitherto obscure Princess's Theatre, and the Queen's manifest approval of his and his wife's endeavours was to serve him in good stead. During the 1850s the Princess's became the most royally favoured playhouse in London, steadily overhauling the St James's. In 1852 the Queen visited it at least thirteen times, in 1854 on ten occasions, and in 1856 on nine. These figures provide the clearest evidence of the success of the plan 'to revive and elevate the English drama which has greatly deteriorated through lack of support by Society', as announced in the Queen's letter to the King of Prussia after the start of the Windsor series.

Her first visit to the Princess's under Kean's management was on 15 February 1851, when she saw the historical piece, *The Templar*. For this first season Kean had struck up a partnership with Mr and Mrs Keeley, a comic team whom the Queen admired enormously, and who had played Launcelot Gobbo and Nerissa in the initial Windsor performance. Again it was the comedian's offstage personality that captivated her:

We dined early, and went to the Princess's Theatre, under the management of Kean and Keeley, who both received us at the door with candles. I had never seen the latter off the stage before, and we could hardly keep our countenances when we saw him walk backwards up a very steep staircase, in constant danger of falling, from Kean's treading upon him. He is very small, fat, and bald.

After this season Kean and Keeley parted company, but this did not mar their understanding, and the Keeleys appeared regularly throughout the Windsor series.

Inevitably the favour shown to Kean, both in entrusting him with responsibility at Windsor, and in bestowing royal approval on his management at the Princess's, provoked criticism and opposition. Foremost in the attack was Douglas Jerrold, who had his own platform in *Lloyd's Weekly Newspaper*, and his own quarrel with Kean. The actor-manager had staged several of Jerrold's plays though not to the author's satisfaction and had turned down several more.

A characteristic onslaught appeared in *Lloyd's* on 13 November 1853, occasioned by the performance at Windsor three days earlier of *Henry V* in which Samuel Phelps (at Kean's suggestion) had played the king:

THE GREAT KEAN MONOPOLY

The Kean monopoly has been broken through. Mr Phelps performed *Henry V* at Windsor Castle on Thursday last. He has been the first to find a northwest passage to the palace. The passage once found, others may quickly follow. The difficulties of the passage no one can conceive, but those who have had to steer through the immense blocks of ice which Mr Charles Kean has thrown in the way of his brother managers . . . He has used this privilege for the glorification of himself as an actor and a manager, until the Queen and the Court have been brought to believe that there was but one English actor and but one English theatre; that actor being Mr Charles Kean, and that theatre being the Princess's!! . . . We hope a dramatic commission will be issued from Windsor Castle (and how proud we shall be if we are nominated to sit upon it!) to inquire into the following questions:

How far the patronage bestowed upon Mr Charles Kean has benefited the drama?

How often he has allowed other managers to perform?—and the number of times those managers have performed in comparison with Charles Kean?

To inquire how often Mr Phelps has performed at Windsor Castle before Thursday evening, November 10th, 1853?

To discover the names of the other tragedians who have played at Windsor Castle, by the kind permission and favour of Mr Charles Kean? . . .

And lastly to state the extent of injury which the English stage would suffer, and whether it would be more weak and ailing than it already is, if Mr Charles Kean were to lose tomorrow the lucrative situation which he at present holds at Court, of 'WET NURSE TO THE BRITISH DRAMA'?[19]

While Jerrold's challenge smacks of self-interest (as well as disrespect for the Crown), his questions can be profitably answered from the statistics of the whole series of Windsor plays, including the years 1859–61 in which Kean took no part. Although he or his wife appeared in twenty performances, a substantial lead over his rivals, with ultimate responsibility and the Princess's Company to call on, this may be judged desirable as well as inevitable. The next highest tally was achieved by Alfred Wigan (thirteen). The Keeleys made eight appearances, and Charles James Mathews played in every season until 1854, and again in 1859–60. When to these names are added frequent appearances by leading actors like Phelps, Buckstone, Harley, Webster, and Robson, it cannot be argued that Kean dominated the Windsor performances to the exclusion of his competitors.

Another objective announced by the Queen in her letter to Frederick William of Prussia fell short of complete achievement. This was her reference to 'a number of performances of classical plays'. In fact the Windsor programmes proved decidedly unbalanced. Shakespeare understandably dominated: thirteen of his plays were performed: *The Merchant of Venice* (twice); *Hamlet; Julius Caesar; Henry IV: Parts I and II; As You Like It; Twelfth Night; King John; Macbeth* (twice); *Henry V; Richard II; The Tempest; Romeo and Juliet.* To these may be added four comedies which could with a little indulgence be termed 'classical': *The Rivals; The School for Scandal; The Critic; The Jealous Wife*, together with four nineteenth-century favourites (*Richelieu; Money; Masks and Faces; Still Waters Run Deep*) which those responsible doubtless judged the best in this kind. These titles, however, account for only twenty-three out of the fifty nights of performance. The majority of the remaining nights were devoted to double-bills of comedies and farces of which even the titles are mostly forgotten. Given the Crown's wish to support the English theatrical profession as a whole (and not merely its 'classical' exponents, as represented by Kean and Phelps), there was little alternative. Performers like Buckstone, the Keeleys, Mathews and Robson rarely appeared in 'classical' plays; their livelihood was the farce, the burlesque, the *comedietta*. The Windsor Theatricals may therefore be judged to have set the royal seal of approval on what the English theatre had to offer, and in so doing to have sustained the standards achieved at that period. They can certainly not be held culpable for failing to bring forward a T. W. Robertson or W. S. Gilbert, still less a Wilde or Shaw, before their time.

The Queen's response to the plays offered her provides a chance to assess her mature dramatic taste. The reactions found in *The Girlhood of Queen Victoria* are those of an impressionable child growing into a young woman. The volumes of the Journal for the 1840s throw far more light on her taste in opera than drama. The Windsor performances opened her eyes to the variety of drama at the playgoer's command, and in giving that variety her approval, she made many of her well-born and -educated subjects similarly aware.

Her reactions to the Shakespeare performances are consistently predictable. There is an unwavering respect and even reverence for his poetry and philosophy, best, if rather oddly, represented by her admiration for that seldom admired piece, *King John*: 'What a noble, splendid Play it is, and *what* a man Shakespeare was! What knowledge of human nature—what language and what poetry—what power of portraying characters!'[20] The very first play in the series produced a similar response:

The play was *The Merchant of Venice*, and the beauties of the language were heard and understood as they hardly can be in a large theatre. Shakespeare's wit, his knowledge of human nature and of the character of man are un-rivalled. I had never seen the play before and much enjoyed it, there are such fine speeches in it.[21]

while the bitterly contested performance of *Julius Caesar* was judged 'such a finely written tragedy, full of beautiful and celebrated speeches'.[22]

On the other hand there is an increasing dissatisfaction with Shakespeare's lack of 'action'. Although the Windsor texts were curtailed—the Queen refers to the omission of the gravedigger scene in *Hamlet* and notes that *Henry IV: Part II* was given 'with some of the parts somewhat expunged and compressed',[23] she still felt that more compression and expunging were called for. Thus in *Henry IV: Part II*: 'The 5th act in which the King discards Falstaff is very fine and striking. Otherwise the play is devoid of all action and only celebrated for the beauty of its language and its humours.' *Henry V*, too, was 'very fine, though I thought it rather heavy, particularly from Phelps's way of impersonating the King'.[24] Even in *As You Like It* 'The poetry and the sense in every line are admirable and make one wonder at the immortal man, who could in the 16th century write such sense and nonsense, which cannot be approached nowadays. Still as a performance I thought it rather heavy.'[25]

When, however, the Queen saw Shakespeare performed at the Princess's, there is no suggestion of 'heaviness' or tedium. The number of visits she and the Prince Consort paid to certain productions is sufficient indication of this. They saw *King John* (1851) and *Richard III* (1854) three times; *The Winter's Tale* (1856), *Richard II* (1857), and *Henry V* (1859) they attended four times. The principles on which Kean produced Shakespeare were in fact exactly calculated to appeal to his royal patrons: his emphasis on spectacle, employing the fullest skills of the scene-painter, costumier, choreographer, and composer, had an immense impact on the Queen, while the 'antiquarianism' of which Kean was so proud, citing scholarly authorities on the playbill, and changing Bohemia in *The Winter's Tale* to Bithynia to justify Shakespeare's reference to its sea-coast, was an enthusiasm after the Prince's own heart.

There seem grounds for concluding that the cramped conditions of the Rubens Room and difficult acoustics of St George's Hall may have been responsible for the Queen's occasional impatience. Certainly there is never any suggestion that Shakespeare at the Princess's was overlong. At her first viewing of *The Winter's Tale* the Journal records:

Though the performance lasted from shortly after 8 to a quarter past 12, we hardly noticed the length of time, for the interest never flagged one minute, and one was led from one more splendid scene to another . . . Albert was in ecstasies, for really the 'mise-en-scène', the beautiful and numerous changes of scenery, the splendid and strictly correct antique costumes, all taken from the best works and models, the excellent grouping of every scene, the care with which every trifle was attended to, made a unique performance.[26]

Whenever the royal party visited the Princess's, the Queen searched eagerly for spectacular moments, and she was rarely disappointed. In *Macbeth* she decided 'the 2 most striking Tableaux are (1) when the murder of Duncan has been discovered, and all the wild men and soldiers rush in with torches, and (2) the last scene, when Macbeth is killed and Malcolm is raised up on a shield, in the old fashion. It was really beautiful.'[27] In *Henry VIII* 'given with the same correctness and splendour as *King John* and *Macbeth*', she judged as the most impressive tableaux 'those of the Banquet, with the entry of the Masquers, and Queen Katherine's dream, with the angels descending on a sunbeam, waving palm branches and holding out to her a crown of the same.'[28] During the 1850s the Queen commissioned numerous water-colour sketches of plays she had particularly enjoyed; Shakespearean highlights at the Princess's dominate the album in which they are preserved in the Royal Library at Windsor.

Despite her undisguised admiration for these spectacular moments, she was not blind to the limitations of Kean's acting in Shakespeare. She was well aware that Ellen Kean excelled her husband in this field. Of *Henry VIII* she notes: 'I do not think Kean's Wolsey very effective, but Mrs Kean was most admirable'.[29] Of his Macbeth she was more charitable than George Henry Lewes who wrote: 'He makes Macbeth ignoble—one whose crime is that of a common murderer, with perhaps a tendency to Methodism',[30] and records generously: 'Both Keans acted very well, but she in particular.'[31]

Throughout his period of office as Director of the Windsor Theatricals Kean and his wife are referred to in the Journal as 'the good Keans'. The Queen relates her first meeting with them as follows: 'After luncheon Mrs Phipps brought Mr and Mrs Kean to see me in the corridor. She is very ladylike and pleasing, and his manner striking and very good. There is so much decision in what he says, and he says it so well,—just as on the stage.'[32] After the first series of plays, the Queen presented Kean with an elegant diamond ring, set in gold with green and red enamel, which unfortunately was subsequently lost, whereupon a wag suggested it would be found stuck in Macready's gizzard. On at least one occasion Kean's loyalty outran his strength:

We dined early and took the 3 eldest children to the Princess's Theatre to see *King John*, arriving just at the beginning of the 2nd act. While the scene between Hubert and Arthur was going on, a messenger came saying that poor Kean, who was looking dreadfully ill and could hardly walk, and who had risen from sick bed to act, had just fainted. They therefore asked permission to close the Play. It was most disappointing for the poor Children; however, *A Model of a Wife* made up for it.[33]

Somehow one feels the poor Children enjoyed *A Model of a Wife* without repining over *King John*.

Whilst the Shakespearean productions were unquestionably his greatest achievement during his tenure of the Princess's, as an actor Kean was happier in a series of 'gentlemanly melodramas', and the Queen and her consort responded no less enthusiastically to these. The success of a string of 'sensation dramas' (which displayed a decided refinement on the earlier English melodrama, such as *Black-Ey'd Susan* or *Luke the Labourer*) marked the emergence in the English theatre of that strain of Romantic *bravura* which Lemaître had flourished for the

Queen in *Trente Ans dans la Vie d'un Joueur* or *Don César de Bazan.*
The royal couple repeatedly visited the Princess's for *Faust and
Marguerite* ('adapted from the French not in the least from Goethe's
glorious *Faust.* The scenery and "mise-en-scène" were beautiful, the
last scene being unparalleled, exquisite and touching'),[34] *Louis XI, The
Courier of Lyons,* and *The Vampire.* In this last the author, Dion
Boucicault, played a vampire with a strong Irish brogue. Nevertheless,
the Queen wrote: 'I can never forget his livid face and fixed look . . . It
quite haunts me.'[35]

Without question the melodrama at the Princess's that made the
biggest impression on her was another Boucicault piece, *The Corsican
Brothers* (adapted from Dumas), with Kean universally admired for his
interpretation of the two Dei Franchi. She first saw it on 28 February
1852, and was captivated by the skilful doubling, the ingenious use of
'the Corsican trap, for the ghost's appearances, and the effect of the
'visions' (through gauze) experienced by the telepathic twins:

The effect of the ghost in the 1st act, with its wonderful management and
entire noiselessness, was quite alarming. The tableau of the Duel, which
Fabien witnesses, almost immediately after the vanishing of the ghost, was
beautifully grouped and quite touching. The whole, lit by blue light and
dimmed with gauze, had an unearthly effect, and was most impressive and
creepy. . . . we both, and indeed everyone, were in admiration at the whole
performance, and much struck by it. We told Kean so, when he accompanied
us downstairs.

So impressed were the royal playgoers that they returned four times
in the next two months. On her fourth visit the Queen wrote: 'To
the Princess's Theatre where we saw my famous *Corsican Brothers,*
and were as usual much interested and impressed with it. It bears seeing
over and over again.'[36] She even sketched the duel tableau in her
Journal, a unique tribute.

This tribute was perhaps as much to a supporting member of the
Princess's Company as to Kean himself or the play. Alfred Wigan, as
the villain Château-Renaud, occupies a striking position in the centre
of the Queen's sketch, while Kean is relegated to a corner. Wigan was
the son of a courier who had escorted many an English milord on the
Grand Tour, and this aristocratic connection seems to have stuck to his
son, who built his career on his French accent and elegant bearing.
The Queen first saw him as Bassanio in the initial Windsor performance of *The Merchant of Venice,* and noted he was 'very gentleman-

like and quiet'.[37] Her interest rapidly grew: in *Hamlet* 'Mr Wigan did the fop exceedingly well, but it is hardly a part'.[38] In *As You Like It* as Orlando 'Mr Wigan was perfect', whereas Kean was merely 'excellent',[39] and even in the uneventful *Henry IV: Part II*: 'The 4th Act between the dying King and the Prince of Wales is magnificent . . . Phelps and Wigan acted extremely well.'[40] In 1854 Wigan left the Princess's to undertake the management of the Olympic, and from that moment the little playhouse in Wych Street was a regular port of call for the Queen. The Olympic Company were also frequently invited to Windsor, and Wigan's contribution to the performances of special concern. In *Money* he was 'quite perfection, nature itself, and so completely the gentleman'.[41] A week later he was asked at no notice at all to play Rolando, the woman-hater, in Tobin's old favourite, *The Honeymoon* (a curious amalgam of *Much Ado About Nothing* and *The Taming of the Shrew*): 'He had only heard at 4 o'clock that he was wanted, and came down at once, though he was not very well and had not acted the part for 2 years. This was very kind and obliging of him, and we had him specially thanked.'[42] Though long forgotten by posterity, Alfred Wigan qualifies for Queen Victoria's list of special favourites, together with the immortal Taglioni, Grisi, and Lind.

His secession from the Princess's was something of a blow for Charles Kean, but far worse awaited him. The break in the Windsor performances during the winter of 1854–5 is explained in the Court Circular for 30 December: 'There will be no theatrical performances or balls at the Castle this season, the rooms usually occupied for that purpose having been fitted up in the most splendid manner for the reception of the Emperor and Empress of the French.' When the series was resumed the next winter, the venue was moved to St George's Hall, with Kean still in charge, and it was here on 5 February 1857 that (unsuspected by him) he gave his last Windsor performance—as Richard II. That summer the Princess Royal became engaged to Prince Frederick William of Prussia, and the wedding was announced for 22 January 1858 in the Chapel Royal. It was decided to hold a series of Command Performances at Her Majesty's as part of the wedding celebrations. Direction of these performances was assigned to John Mitchell, who had run a successful theatre ticket agency in Bond Street for many years, and was responsible for the French seasons at the St James's. Charles Kean and the Princess's Company did not participate.

Behind these facts doubtless lie many conflicting forces. From the

Court's point of view it was desirable to hold the performances in a large London theatre. None of the Windsor State Rooms would have been remotely suitable. Her Majesty's was available and appropriate. To have invited Kean to direct the series at the Princess's (not a large theatre in any case) would have smacked of favouritism. Lastly, and most English reason of all, Mitchell undertook to organize the performances as a commercial venture at his own risk.

Whatever the full story behind this decision, Kean was mortally offended. Mitchell invited him to appear with his wife and company in *Macbeth*. He refused on the grounds that the invitation should have come from Phipps:

If this is your speculation, Mr Mitchell, as a matter of business I am justified in declining. If the Court were interested in it, as a matter of courtesy, in consideration of the position I have held for so many years as director of Her Majesty's private theatricals, I should assuredly have received some personal communication through the usual channel.[43]

The invitation was therefore transferred to Samuel Phelps, who accepted. On the night in question (19 January) Kean played Hamlet at the Princess's. A crowded house gave him an ovation, and he replied in decidedly aggressive terms:

It would be affectation in me to pretend not to understand the motives which have influenced this particular excitement, and it is another convincing instance, in addition to the many I have already received, that when a public man acts in a conscientious and upright manner, the public will always afford him their sympathy and support.[44]

That, following this speech, he was not invited to resume direction of the Windsor Theatricals is less surprising than that the Queen and Prince Albert continued to patronize the Princess's as generously afterwards as before. They saw *King Lear* three times that summer, and *Henry V* (Kean's swan-song at his own theatre) four times in 1859. Following a visit to the latter the Queen wrote to her eldest daughter in Germany: 'I wish you could have been with us to see *Henry V* which is quite as fine as your beloved *Richard II*.'[45] The entire incident exposes the hothouse jealousies of the theatre world, and stresses the wisdom of confining the series as a whole to the theatrical backwaters of Windsor.

In the event, the performances at Her Majesty's afforded the Queen little pleasure, but whether she was distressed by the controversy surrounding them (widely reported in the Press) or distracted by her duties as mother of the bride is open to question. In any case the audience was rather more interested in itself than what happened onstage: 'The whole theatre was decorated with flowers, and nearly half the House on one side thrown into one box, prettily decorated, with the Concert Room as ante-room. Here we all sat in a wonderful row of Royalties.'[46] On the contentious 19 January the Queen, who had arrived late, was clearly not in a receptive mood: 'The performance of *Macbeth* perfectly atrocious, Phelps and Miss Helen Faucit indescribably bad and slow . . . The performance lasted till a little before 1. Much too long!' On 21 January Balfe's *Rose of Castile* pleased her more—'rather pretty, light music', but she 'only saw two acts of it', and it was 'followed by a Farce, called *Boots at the Swan*, rather stupid and too broad'. Two nights later *La Sonnambula* escaped censure, but there was 'also a bad Cantata and an allegorical Ballet'. Altogether Her Majesty did not enjoy herself at Her Majesty's during these performances.

Meanwhile Kean was licking his wounds. In the account-book his stage-manager kept, he added in his own hand:[47]

Loss By Windsor Theatricals

On nights that the theatre was closed	420	0	0
On nights when weak plays were substituted	381	0	0
Traveling (*sic*) expenses to Osborne (5 times)	50	0	0
Expenses at Windsor, unpaid (36 times)	108	0	0
19 nights of Superintendence (not acting 24 times)	475	0	0
17 nights of Superintendence (acting 15 times)	255	0	0
	£1689	0	0

Not all of this is readily explicable. One possible clue may be found in an expectation, shared by Kean and his wife, that his endeavours at Windsor would be rewarded by a knighthood, a development regularly predicted in some sections of the Press during the early years of the Windsor series.

It may well be that the stresses attached to these wedding celebrations discouraged those responsible from reviving the Windsor Theatricals for almost two years. There were no performances there in 1858–9, and the remaining seasons struck a distinctly muted note. Kean had disqualified himself, and rather than invite one of his rivals to succeed him, the summons went out to William Bodham Donne, a classical scholar and essayist, whose connection by marriage with the Kemble family had resulted in his appointment as Examiner of Plays to the Lord Chamberlain. It was scarcely qualification enough for the delicate assignment he now faced, and he seems to have found the theatrical temperament mysterious and maddening. One of his first approaches, to Charles Kean, was predictably rebuffed; as he reported to Phipps: 'I yesterday received a reply to my "private" application to Mr Charles Kean. He informs me that Mrs Kean and himself are fully engaged until June 1860 and that consequently they cannot have the honour of appearing early in the New Year at Windsor Castle.'[48] Another early move was to propose a pay-rise for the performers, who had hitherto received twice their usual fee for playing at Windsor. The Sadler's Wells Company, he told Phipps,

will be perfectly satisfied and much gratified also, if they are paid for the evening on which the Windsor Plays are to be represented, besides their ordinary salary, twice the amount—i.e. one third more than they have hitherto received.

On looking through the Tariff I find that this will not increase the expenditure by more than £20; and since Mr Kean was paid for his acting, as well as allowed for closing his Theatre, and as you now have an *unsalaried* Director, the difference will be diminished.[49]

Donne was soon made aware that the Queen took a very personal interest in the plays selected. One of his suggestions, Tom Taylor's *An Unequal Match*, did not find favour:

Osborne 7 December 1859

The Queen must ask Sir C. Phipps *not* to *settle* definitely about what *Plays* for Windsor. On reflection she thinks the 3rd Act of *The Unequal Match* too offensive on account of the ridicule it throws on German life—the Soldiers of a small German country etc.—to have at Court. Any foreign Prince *might* arrive, and we should have suddenly to alter the Play.[50]

A week later another proposal, *House and Home*, was met with a counter-suggestion:

Osborne 13 December 1859

Would Sir C. Phipps desire a copy of *House and Home* to be sent? We think *The Hunchback* might do instead of *An Unequal Match*. Miss Sedgwick acts *Julia* admirably—and if there are any objectionable pages or Scenes, surely they might be omitted?[51]

This royal censorship was a feature of the Windsor performances from the very beginning. After the initial staging of *The Merchant of Venice* Phipps had written to Charles Kean: 'I must remind you in time that it is necessary that I should see the prompt copies of *Used Up* and *Box and Cox* before they are performed—although I feel pretty sure that there is nothing objectionable in either.'[52] A further problem had arisen with regard to this production of *Used Up*, in which the actor Henry Howe played a blacksmith. Phipps learnt with alarm that he represented his craft by rolling up his sleeves, and remonstrated. 'However, when the matter was referred to Her Majesty, she graciously expressed a desire that the part should be played in the ordinary way.'[53]

Only very rarely did the 'normal channels' fail. There was always a danger that a good joke in French might turn out a bad joke in English. After a double bill of *The Captain of the Watch* and *The Windmill* in 1853, the Queen observed: 'Both translated from the French, but a little "équivoque" for our theatre here. The 2nd is more "équivoque" than the other, without any of its merits. It did not suit the Keeleys, though they acted very well.'[54] A year earlier, another double bill (*Not a Bad Judge* and *The Lottery Ticket*) left Charles James Mathews exposed to criticism: 'The 2nd piece, though laughable, is a vulgar farce which did not come well after the other.'[55] It cannot be too strongly stressed, however, that the Queen was the most responsive of audiences. 'We were all in fits of laughter' is her regular reaction to comedy, and her favourite comedians like Buckstone, Harley and Robson, were 'ridiculous beyond belief', 'perfection', and '*impayable*'. What above all she required of a play was thrills or laughter —preferably both—and she rewarded with her appreciation those who gave her what she asked.

Not surprisingly the bewildered Donne fell back on established companies in proven favourites, notably Buckstone and the Haymarket team, Webster from the Adelphi, and the Olympic Company. The final programme of the 1859–60 season included Charles James Mathews in *A Bachelor of Arts*, his last appearance before the sovereign who had relished his mastery of the art of comedy for a quarter of a century. The only classical element in the programmes was provided by Samuel Phelps and his Sadler's Wells colleagues. They gave *Romeo and Juliet* in 1859, which the Queen approved: 'Miss Heath was a charming Juliet, and Mr Robinson, a new actor, a very good Romeo. He has a fine voice, and will be still better when he has given up some conventionalities.'[56] This was followed in 1861 by

Richelieu ('. . . Had not seen the piece for 22 years.')[57] Some of the other performances were more notable for offstage drama. In January 1860 the Haymarket played Sheridan Knowles's *The Hunchback*, at the Queen's behest, but she was chiefly concerned with one of the audience, the Prime Minister: 'Lord Palmerston had such a fall in going across the steps, but picked himself up again very actively.'[58]

A suggestion that something loftier would enhance the Windsor programmes seems to have circulated. Charles Kean eventually brought himself to comment to his successor on this subject: 'I am now convinced that these Royal theatricals have done much good and will continue to do so, and the benefit would still be increased if the Royal liking went more in favour of high class drama than for farce and trifles.'[59] Donne responded, not very realistically, by offering to translate Schiller's *Wallenstein* for performance in the 1861–2 season. It was, of course, one thing to translate the play, and quite another to persuade a manager of its viability. On 25 February he wrote to Phipps:

As regards *Wallenstein*, with a view to Windsor, I am busy reducing the 2 parts: *Die Piccolomini* and *Wallenstein's Tod*—into one drama.
Phelps says: 'If you can make me a play that will run at Sadler's Wells, after its introduction at Windsor—*good*, but if it would not run as a public entertainment, *not so good*, since I and my company would not have time to study such a drama for one representation.' Phelps failing, I know not where to look; for, as Quince says of Bottom the Weaver: 'He is the properest man in all Athens' for the principal role. Kean could not, and I fancy would not take *Wallenstein*: indeed whenever I have offered him an evening at Windsor he has replied rather curtly.[60]

Phipps remained convinced of the virtues of Schiller, but perhaps remembering the unpleasant recriminations with Charles Kean, would not press the point:

Phelps is, like all actors, short-sighted, I think, even to his own interest. It is very probable that it might be difficult to make *Wallenstein* an attractive play to 'the multitude'—but the fact of its being produced at Windsor Castle, especially for Miss Heath and him to play in, would raise them both professionally in public opinion—and what with the Classical set who would be curious to see the poem on the Stage; and the Royalty-hunters, who would go to see anything that has been acted at Windsor, it will be certain to draw houses for a certain time. However, he must do nothing unwillingly or that would give him a power afterwards of saying: I lost by the Windsor Plays.[61]

12 *Above Les Huguenots* at Covent Garden, 1855.
The only contemporary opera of which the Queen
commissioned sketches.

13 and 14 *Overleaf* The Royal Family presents (above)
Das Hahnenschlag (below) *Athalie*. '. . . dearest Albert, sitting
near me, directing everything.'

Hannchen   Margaretta   Peter   Fritz   Wilhelm   Lischen
Alice   Vicky   Affie   Bertie   Leiniken   Louis

In the event, fate took the matter out of both men's hands. The last Windsor performance (*The Overland Route* by the Haymarket Company) took place on 31 January 1861. Although the Prince Consort's health was far from good, the Queen and he attended the theatre a number of times in the early part of that year. But on 16 March the Duchess of Kent died. The period of mourning prescribed for the sovereign's mother would have precluded theatre visits in any case, but the Queen experienced a deep sense of loss and unhappiness, and withdrew to Osborne. Her appearances during the London season that summer were few, and her appearances at the theatre non-existent. Plans for a Windsor season were postponed. Perhaps, if she recovered her spirits in the autumn, something might be arranged. It was not to be. The Queen had paid her last visit to a theatre.

5

Family Favourites

The success of the Windsor Theatricals over more than a decade greatly encouraged the flagging spirits of the English theatre. The celebration of native arts and crafts which Prince Albert conceived and tended to fruition in the Great Exhibition of 1851 inaugurated an era in the dramatic world which, if less spectacular than the jewels of the Crystal Palace, nevertheless saw English actors and playwrights shine with a steadily increasing light. One outstanding example of this has already been examined: Charles Kean's management of the Princess's Theatre, which with its antiquarian Shakespeare and 'gentlemanly melodrama' brought to Oxford Street much of the prestige Drury Lane and Covent Garden had lost when they abandoned 'legitimate' drama.

By the mid '50s the increase in royal patronage of English theatrical enterprise was becoming manifest. The Queen had acquired the habit of totting up at the end of the year her record of theatre visits, and her (not wholly systematic or self-explanatory) notes are preserved in the Royal Archives in a handsome 'blotter', on the cover of which she has pasted a portrait of her *Puritani* tenor, Rubini. In 1854 she calculated she had been

25 times to the Play
13 times to the French play (and *opéra comique*)
14 times to the New Opera [*i.e.* Covent Garden]

but by 1856 she estimates twenty-seven visits to the Play, nine to the Opera (Covent Garden and Her Majesty's), none to the French play.
The significance of the decline in visits to the opera will be con-

sidered later. Here it is the virtual disappearance of visits to the French companies at the St James's which demands attention, especially when contrasted with the rising total (twenty-five in 1854, twenty-seven in 1856) of visits to English-speaking theatres. Undoubtedly the decline in the standards of visiting French companies contributed to this. In 1859 the Queen could write to her eldest daughter: 'We have had none [good companies] since '54.'[1] Insofar as the Court preserved an interest in continental drama, that interest switched from French to German and Italian visitors. In 1852 and 1853 Emil Devrient brought his Dresden Company to London, where society received him with the same enthusiasm that had greeted Rachel. His repertoire made few concessions to light entertainment. The Queen saw him in *Egmont*, complete with Beethoven's incidental music:

It is a fine play, full of beautiful language and feelings, and very true in its political bearings, but with so little action that it is heavy. The acting was very good. Emil Devrient is a fine, noble actor ... The applause was great and the House immensely full.[2]

The two eldest children were required to accompany their parents to *Don Carlos* and were 'extremely attentive',[3] while the Queen persevered with *Kabale und Liebe*, *Hamlet* (in German), and most importantly *Faust*:

We dined early and went to the St James's Theatre to see Goethe's great and wonderful Tragedy of *Faust*. It was in 6 acts and though necessarily much curtailed, it lasted till 12. Having never read it before, I can hardly be a fit judge of it, but I mean to study it well now. For Philosophy, depth of feeling, and beauty of reasoning, it has no equal, but I could not understand the last part or follow it well.[4]

As an earnest of her intention to master Goethe's *magnum opus*, the Queen invited Devrient to give a solo performance, including extracts from *Faust*, at Buckingham Palace, 'a great treat and an intellectually elevating one'.[5] The following year she saw Devrient and the Dresden Company in *Wilhelm Tell* and *Donna Diana*.

Three years later Adelaide Ristori conquered the London theatre. Rachel had now abandoned her English admirers for American audiences, and tragic acting in London was sustained on the distaff side mainly by Ellen Tree, a true artiste but an increasingly solid figure, especially as she insisted on retaining her crinoline, whatever the part and however dedicated to 'correct' costume her husband might be.

The Queen saw Ellen as Hermione in *The Winter's Tale* (complete with starched petticoats under her *chiton*) several times in April and May 1856, but on 9 June she experienced tragic acting of a higher intensity at the Lyceum:

We dined early with Vicky and Fritz, and went with them to the Lyceum to see the celebrated Italian 'Tragédienne', Madame Ristori. The tragedy was *Medea*, translted from the French of Gouvé, a fearful subject, and not a good piece, but *such* acting as her's I have never seen. She throws Rachel into the shade. She is a magnificent looking person, very tall and thin, with a commanding appearance and fine regular features. Her voice is most beautiful, and in the touching scenes inexpressibly moving. Every attitude and action is like that of an antique statue!

The Queen also saw Ristori in *Maria Stuarda* (from Schiller) and Alfieri's *Rosamunda*. 'Fritz' was of course Prince Frederick William of Prussia whom Vicky was to marry less than two years later. *Medea*, in whatever language, seems something of a baptism of fire for their courtship.

The pattern of royal operagoing in the 1850s was largely shaped by the challenge to Her Majesty's of the resuscitated Covent Garden. The building had been ambitiously remodelled in 1847, and the theatre styled 'The New Italian Opera'. Soon after its reopening the Queen and Prince Albert heard *Semiramide* there, and warmly approved: 'The House, beautifully fitted up, looks like a foreign Theatre, such as La Scala, Albert says. The Orchestra, conducted by Costa, was admirable. *Semiramide* was beautifully got up—very fine scenery, decorations, dresses etc.'[6] In fact the Queen contrasted Covent Garden's splendid new appearance with some ill-judged attempts to brighten Her Majesty's the previous year: 'The House is quite newly done up, but I find the yellow very glaring.'[7]

Her reference to Covent Garden under the musical direction of Michael Costa indicates the civil war raging between Alfred Bunn and Lumley at Her Majesty's. As has been seen, Bunn succeeded in enticing not only Costa but all the principal singers from Her Majesty's with the exception of Luigi Lablache. Lumley was able to counter by engaging Jenny Lind, and for the next three seasons the two houses fought for the patronage of London's opergoers. But after Lind's retirement from the stage in 1849, Her Majesty's rapidly lost ground and was more often closed than open. The statistics in the Queen's blotter confirm this; after 1851 she records only nine visits in all to Her Majesty's, compared with an average of ten visits a year to Covent Garden.

The most prestigious of these occasions was the performance of *Fidelio* on 19 April 1855 in honour of Napoleon III and his Empress. The State visit of the Emperor of the French had been reluctantly approved by the Queen (who resented his replacement of Louis Philippe) and by Prince Albert, 'who, you know, is anything but favourable to the French'. His stay at Windsor had presented various diplomatic problems—the Waterloo Chamber, for example, had to be hastily rechristened the Portrait Gallery. Nevertheless the exotic personalities of both Napoleon and Eugénie cast their spell over the Queen, and the visit was an undoubted success, not least the excursion to Covent Garden, though it began badly:

Just as we were ready to go, the Emperor upset his cup of coffee over his cocked hat, which caused great amusement. We drove with an Escort. Never did I see such enormous crowds at night—all in highest good humour. We literally drove through a *sea* of human beings, cheering and pressing the carriage. The streets were beautifully illuminated, and many letters 'N.E.' and 'V.A.' were to be seen, which the Emperor remarked curiously enough made Neva, the River on which St Petersburg is built. When we reached the Opera Albert, as usual, led the Empress, and the Emperor me, and when we entered I led the Emperor forward, making it as clear as I could that *he* was the principal person on this occasion. The applause generally was very marked, or very marked for *him*. 'Partant pour la Syrie' was 1st played, and then 'God Save the Queen'. The 2nd act of *Fidelio* was given. The whole stage was opened out, and 2 military Bands stationed on it, which had a very fine effect. Back home we came, with the same immense crowds.

Less than a year after this State visit Covent Garden was in ashes. A *bal masqué* on the night of 5 March 1856 led to a fire which brought about its almost total destruction, and with it such treasures as Sheridan's manuscript of *The School for Scandal* and Weber's autographed score of *Oberon*. The distress of the proprietors and the difficulties of the fire brigade cannot have been eased next day by the sequence of royal sightseers. The Queen and the Princess Royal arrived about 4 o'clock in the afternoon, and were conducted round by the lessee, Frederick Gye, who had arrived back from Paris that morning to face up to the disaster.

They were conducted through a low doorway in one of the internal walls, to a spot near what had been the position of Her Majesty's private box, from which they obtained an excellent view of the ruins, and were able to form an adequate conception of the vast area originally covered by the building, and the melancholy scene of desolation and destruction which it presented.[8]

Half an hour later Prince Albert arrived, and was similarly shown round by the stout-hearted lessee. Sightseers the following day included the Duke of Cambridge (the Queen's cousin), the Prince of Wales and his tutor, and Prince Alfred. For a brief period the ruins of Covent Garden seem to have competed with the Tower of London and Westminster Abbey as a tourist attraction.

Whilst Covent Garden was rebuilding, the Lyceum was hastily brought into commission as an opera-house. It is noticeable that the Queen chose to patronize the stop-gap Lyceum rather than the long-established house in the Haymarket, although Benjamin Lumley seized the opportunity offered him and immediately reopened Her Majesty's. The Queen returned to her once favourite theatre on one occasion in 1856 and twice in 1857. Significantly, in the lists she kept during these years, the total for her visits to Her Majesty's is calculated only up to *La Sonnambula* on 29 May 1852, her 350th evening there. Perhaps the house held too many precious memories for her to accept declining standards. On the other hand, during the closure of Covent Garden she paid thirteen visits to the Lyceum, where she saw daringly new works like *Rigoletto*, as well as old favourites like *Don Giovanni* and *Les Huguenots*. Following the reopening of Covent Garden under the stalwart Frederick Gye on 15 May 1858, the Queen renewed her loyalty to that house. In 1859 she attended ten performances there. Amongst the leading singers were Grisi, idol of the Queen's girlhood, and Mario, the Italian marquis she had married. Both were approaching fifty, and their retirement, repeatedly announced, could not long be delayed. Grisi's came in 1861. What was less expected was the Queen's last visit to Covent Garden on 25 February of that year, to see an old favourite, Auber's *Domino Noir*. The loss of her husband was to accomplish what the fire had signally failed to do.

One factor which distinguished royal theatregoing in the 1850s from the previous decade was the growth—both in numbers and age —of the Royal Family. By 1851 the Queen and Prince Albert were the parents of seven children, and only Prince Leopold and Princess Beatrice had still to appear. The children clearly inherited their parents' love of the theatre. Entries in the Queen's blotter, such as 'with 2 eldest Boys and 3 youngest Girls', multiply in the mid '50s. Prince Arthur in particular seems to have developed a taste for playgoing at a remarkably early age. 'With Arthur (birthday), Helena, and Louise' appears against *Grimshaw, Bagshaw, and Bradshaw* at the Haymarket on 1 May 1856, when he was just six. Sometimes the Royal Family over-flowed the Royal Box. 'Dined earlier and went to the Princess's to a Pantomime' (*The Miller and his Men* suitably transmogrified) is the Queen's entry for 21 February 1854:

The Boys were in a box below us. The Children were delighted, and the evolutions of the 80 little children, none older than 6 and some only 3, as the Scots Fusiliers, were very pretty. Lord Aberdeen, Lord J. Russell, and Lord Palmerston were represented. 7 people dressed as ladies, turned into chairs, which was really marvellous.

Child performers always found a sympathetic response in the Queen. The Terry family were established favourites: an early Windsor performance, *King John*, was notable in this respect: 'The character of poor little "Arthur" was most touchingly and beautifully acted by Miss Kate Terry, a little girl of 9 years old. The scene between Arthur and Hubert was heartrending.'[9] The Victorian stage convention of casting actresses as small boys is no longer to the playgoer's taste, but the Queen delighted in it. Kate Terry's sister came to her notice in *A Midsummer Night's Dream* at the Princess's: 'Miss Ellen Terry (about 9 years old) played the part of "Robin" delightfully, and "Pease-blossom", "Mustard" [*sic*], etc., were represented by darling little children.'[10] Pantomime was another opening for child performers; indeed some of the glimpses the Queen's Journal affords suggest lamentable exploitation of the very young. Mention has been made of 'the evolutions of the 80 little Children, none older than 6' in *The Miller and his Men* in 1854. Two years earlier, in *Cherry and Fair Star*, also at the Princess's, Kate Terry seems to have been the oldest child in the company:

Little Kate Terry acted the principal part in the Introduction very nicely, though suffering from a sore throat. There was a little fairy who appeared for a few minutes, actually kneeling in front of the stage, lifting up her arms, who was quite a fat Baby, decidedly younger than little Arthur.[11]

Since little Arthur would then be one year ten months old, the fat

Baby must literally have been taking her first steps on the stage. Even General Tom Thumb, the famous American dwarf, aroused maternal instincts in the royal breast. He was invited to appear at Buckingham Palace in 1844, but the Queen experienced more pity than wonder: 'One cannot help feeling very sorry for the poor little thing, and wishing he could be properly cared for, for the people who shew him off tease him a good deal, I should think.'[12]

'With Vicky' appears regularly in the Queen's list of plays attended. Clearly she did not enjoy the theatre without at least one of her family, and if Prince Albert was prevented from accompanying her, she turned naturally enough to her eldest daughter. The Princess Royal became a dedicated playgoer, and after her marriage her correspondence with her mother is rich in theatrical exchanges. The Queen encouraged her to see *Faust*, notwithstanding its brutalities: 'You need not be afraid of seeing *Faust*; I am as bad and shy as anyone, matron as I am, about these things—and it is so beautiful that really one does not feel put out by it. I advise you to see it, dear.'[13] Surprisingly enough, she is less encouraging on the subject of *The Merry Wives of Windsor*, even in German: 'By the by you went to see the *Merry Wives*; you must have found it very coarse; even I have never had the courage to see it —having always been told how very coarse it was—for your adored Shakespeare is dreadful in that respect and many things have to be left out in many of his plays.'[14]

Another dramatic *genre* of which the Queen had grave suspicions was the Latin play at Westminster School. She strongly resented the limitation of the audience to the male sex, and could only attribute this to one cause. Nevertheless her husband regularly attended, and even took his elder sons with him. His wife confided her disapproval to their daughter: 'Dear Papa is still not quite well—he went yesterday evening with Bertie (who understood not a word of it) to see the Westminster boys act one of their (very improper) Latin plays.'[15] One non-professional group of players whose performances the Queen could and did attend was that organized by Charles Dickens and comprising many of his colleagues. She and the Prince saw them in *Not So Bad As We Seem*, the piece specially written by Bulwer-Lytton, in 1851:

The Duke of Devonshire kindly lent his house for the performance, all the tickets being worth £5. The rooms and the little theatre were beautifully arranged, we 4 sitting in a sort of little box. All acted on the whole well, Dickens (the celebrated author) admirably, and Mr Jerrold, a funny little man who writes in *Punch*, extremely well. Mr Lemon was also very good, and Mr Egg looked very picturesque—like Schiller and Milton. The dresses and scenery were beautiful.[16]

The play itself was 'full of cleverness though rather too long'. More to her taste was a subsequent offering by the group, given at the Gallery of Illustration in Regent Street, later to be the cradle of both Gilbert's and Sullivan's theatrical careers. The play on this occasion was

an admirable Melodrama in 3 acts, by Wilkie Collins, called *The Frozen Deep*, a tale by the Northern Arctic Expedition, most interesting, intensely dramatic, and most touching and moving at the end. The Play was admirably acted by Charles Dickens (whose representation of Richard Wardour was beyond all praise and not to be surpassed), his 3 daughters and sons, Mark Lemon the author, etc.[17]

The pattern of the Queen's playgoing in the 1850s was shared between old loyalties and new enthusiasms, the most important of the latter being for Charles and Ellen Kean at the Princess's. One actor whom she had supported, though sometimes under protest, from her youth, retired early in the decade. Macready gave his farewell performance as Macbeth on 26 February 1851 at Drury Lane, and withdrew to decent Dorset, where he could be what he really enjoyed, a gentleman. Three weeks before this final exit the Queen saw him at the Haymarket as Lear:

It was Macready's *last* performance of that part. At the beginning, when King Lear's daughters use him so ill, and when he curses them, Macready much over did the part, but from the time the King becomes mad to the last, he acted very well. The scene where he recovers consciousness and recognises Cordelia is very fine, and the last scene, when he brings her in dead in his arms, mourning over her, is most touching and painful.[18]

There was always respect, never love, in the Queen's response to Macready's acting, but then he was not an actor who always inspired love in his audience.

The Haymarket itself was a theatre of which she had long been fond, and in this decade, first under Webster and then under Buckstone, she increased her patronage of it. On the whole, the less ambitious its programme, the more she enjoyed herself there. Compared with the Princess's, its classical productions were commonplace. In 1855 the theatre ventured on one of its infrequent stagings of Shakespeare, marked by freak casting in the shape of an American tragedienne as Romeo: 'Miss Cushman took the part of Romeo, and no one would ever have imagined she was a woman, her figure and voice being so masculine, but her face was very plain. Her acting is not pleasing, though clever, and she entered well into the character, bringing out so forcibly its impetuosity.'[19] Charlotte Cushman was not one of the Queen's idols. The previous year she had ruined a production of an old friend:

We dined early, and went with Vicky etc. to the Haymarket, where *Guy Mannering* was given, which I had not seen for 20 years, I being then 1 year older than Vicky is now. A pretty piece, fairly well acted, with the exception of 'Meg Merrilees' which Miss Cushman acted in quite a wrong, unconvincing manner. She looked like the most frightful witch in *Macbeth* and was quite hideous to behold, with a very unpleasant manner.[20]

On the other hand the farces and extravaganzas with which the Haymarket filled out the bill warmed the Queen's heart. The company were essentially a family playing for families (including the Royal Family), as some of the titles presented suggest: *Keeley Worried by Buckstone; Buckstone's Adventure with a Polish Princess; Mr Buckstone's Ascent of Mount Parnassus; Mr Buckstone's Voyage Round the Globe; Mr Buckstone at Home*. The Haymarket bill was as varied and variable as any London theatre's. One item much loved by the Queen were the Spanish dancers who appeared there frequently between 1854 and 1856. With the decline of Her Majesty's she sorely missed the great exponents of ballet she had once worshipped. The Spaniards provided not perhaps a substitute so much as an alternative: 'We dined alone and went to the Haymarket, where we saw a Ballet with Spanish dancers, in fact no Ballet, but only a succession of lively and spirited dances, which were charmingly executed by 6 men and 6 women, besides the 2 principal dancers, Senora Perla Maria and Senor Ruiz. They are the best dancers we have ever seen.'[21] Their subsequent appearances could always be relied on to fill the Royal Box.

At least one new play presented at the Haymarket during these years won the Queen's whole-hearted approval, and established itself firmly in the Victorian repertoire. *Masks and Faces*, a back-stage story in which Peg Woffington was the heroine, and Kitty Clive, Colley Cibber, and James Quin all appeared, was first played there on 20 November 1852. The Queen saw it three months later, and declared roundly: 'The piece is full of light and shade, at times lively and full of humour, again pathetic and very affecting. The moral and feelings, too, are excellent ... Webster as Triplet, the poor starving Poet and Painter, as well as Mrs Stirling [as Peg Woffington] acted their parts beautifully.'[22] When Webster moved to the Adelphi the following year, he took Tom Taylor and Charles Reade's piece with him. The Queen (breaking new ground) saw the play again there, and also at Windsor in the very last season.

The Haymarket was a firm favourite amongst theatres, and Charles James Mathews and Madame Vestris were firm favourites amongst players. In the late 1840s and '50s their star—or at least the lady's— was waning, but the Queen did not desert them on that account. In 1847 they had taken over the lease of the Lyceum, a larger house than suited their style, and although persevering with the *comediettas* which showed off their delicacy of touch, found themselves increasingly dependent on pantomime and melodrama. The Royal Family patronized their pantomimes devotedly, and the Queen's Journal pays eloquent tribute to the spectacular effects (which their author, Planché, came to resent as bitterly as two hundred years earlier Ben Jonson had accused Inigo Jones of taking over his masques). In *The Island of Jewels* the costumes were 'quite dazzling, and the last scene really one of the prettiest, most brilliant imaginable'.[23] Even more breath-taking was *The Prince of the Happy Land*: 'The last scene is quite gorgeous, a gigantic Pineapple unfolds at each rib, which opens and a fairy glittering in silver and lit up with brilliant lights appears. Children are at the topmost point, surrounded by blue and red lights, which give a most dazzling effect.'[24] But the Queen was also aware, with Planché, of the danger of smothering the subject in scenery. *King Charming* was 'not very clever, but gorgeous as to the dresses and scenery',[25] and even *The Prince of the Happy Land* 'too long, with much tiresome and bad singing'.[26]

If these reservations were made of the Lyceum pantomimes, in which Vestris and Mathews let their designer, William Beverly, call the tune, there was greater cause for reserve over the melodramas with which they tried to fill the wide Lyceum stage and increasingly empty auditorium. The Queen appreciated the finesse of the two stars in *The Game of Speculation* (from Balzac) which she saw at the Lyceum twice in 1852 and commanded for Windsor in 1853. But she detected the writing on the wall when these two light comedians staged *A Chain of Events* (from Scribe)—'a very long piece in 8 acts, freely translated from the French. But it was neither amusing nor interesting, from the total want of unity, the terrible length, and childishness of the dialogue.'[27] The shadows deepened over her two long-standing favourites. Vestris was dying; Mathews was bankrupt again, though his friends rallied round to keep his enterprise afloat. Yet his royal patron did not abandon him; on 9 March 1855 she saw him in *Take Away that Girl*. A fortnight later his creditors closed in on him and the Lyceum. In the next eighteen months he was thrown into a debtors' gaol and his greatly-loved partner died.

If old favourites were in shadow, new favourites shared the sunshine with the Queen and the public. Alfred Wigan used the springboard of his success with Charles Kean to vault into the seat of management at the Olympic, where once the Queen had marvelled at Mathews's gentlemanly ways. She hastened to give Wigan her support. 'We dined alone and then went to the Olympic, where we saw some excellent acting. It is Mr A. Wigan's Theatre, and a private entrance has been made.'[28] But a shock awaited her. The idol off-stage proved to have—not feet of clay but a head without hair. 'Wigan received us —very gentlemanlike and good-looking, but completely bald.' Love is not love which alters when it alteration finds, and the Queen was loyal, if shaken. She applauded Wigan as Achille Talma Dufourd, the old French actor whose daughter's début provided the plot, as well as the title, of *The First Night*: 'a "chef d'oeuvre", every attitude, every expression so finished and so thoroughly and characteristically French. He kept me in fits of laughter, and yet there were again quite pathetic moments. Poor Wigan himself is very unwell, having to lie down for an hour before he acts, and he is to go away for a month.'[29]

When the following year Wigan put on *Still Waters Run Deep*, not only the Queen but her husband took the play to their hearts. Catch-phrases from Tom Taylor's dialogue evidently entered the royal vocabulary. In a letter to Vicky dated 4 May 1859 the Queen writes: 'Now goodbye and God bless you, my dearest, and as Papa says (the policeman says it to Hawkesley in *Still Waters Run Deep*) "Keep up your pecker, that's right" meaning keep up your spirits and don't be downhearted.'[30] Since the policeman appears only briefly in the last minutes of the play, this suggests a close acquaintance with the text. Certainly it made a wholly favourable impression when the Queen and her husband first saw it:

To the Olympic, where we saw the whole of *Still Waters Run Deep*, which really is admirably written and acted. Wigan is perfect as Mildmay, who is a very fine character, and Emery as the old twaddling father. Mrs Wigan as the domineering aunt, Mr G. Vining as the infamous adventurer etc., all looked and acted well. Albert was delighted with it.[31]

The play remained a royal favourite—a Command Performance was given at Windsor the following January, and when Wigan joined the Adelphi Company in 1859, the Queen and her husband saw it there. Her reactions are at once predictable and surprising—enthusiasm for Wigan's performance was to be expected, but there is no hint that the theme was by contemporary standards 'daring'. Indeed the Journal describes it after the Windsor performance as 'that pretty piece'.[32] Yet the French original (*Le Gendre* by Charles Bernard) predicates a mother who discovers her married daughter encouraging the attentions of a libertine with whom she has herself been involved, and who takes her daughter's place at a midnight assignation with him to save the marriage. That Taylor himself was aware of the dangers of this situation for an English audience is clear from his altering the relationship of the two women to aunt and niece. The hero of the piece is, however, John Mildmay, the husband—mild of manner but mighty in mind, and this part was Wigan's triumph and the Queen's joy. Besides, 'Albert was delighted with it'.

Wigan was not the only member of the company who drew the Royal Family to the Olympic. Increasingly the Journal makes mention of 'the new actor, Robson'. Frederick Robson was an unusual addition to the Queen's theatrical portrait gallery. His background was as different from that of Old Etonian Charles Kean or the French polish of Wigan as can be imagined; his early experience was in the (still suspect, and with good grounds) music hall, singing songs like 'Villikins and his Dinah'. But he combined grotesquerie with an extraordinary mixture of comic and pathetic appeal, and rapidly became a major star in the Olympic constellation. His uniquely blended gifts were at their most powerful in burlesque and extravaganza, where he simultaneously parodied and transcended the part he was playing. The Queen does not appear to have seen his Medea, which Ristori (on whose interpretation it was based) declared better than her own, but another of his historic performances she describes as 'a very droll and clever Extravaganza called *The Yellow Dwarf*, in which Robson enacts the part of the Yellow Dwarf most remarkably, and looks too horrid, though he sings and dances delightfully, contriving to have the most crooked legs imaginable.'[33] She saw Robson frequently, both at the Olympic and at Windsor, and though she admired him in many of his best-known 'straight' roles (*Boots at the Swan; The Porter's Knot; Daddy Hardacre*) she particularly relished his singing and dancing. Thus after *The Discreet Princess*, which she saw several times in 1856, she admits: 'His song, terminating with the refrain "Diddle doo, diddle dum" quite haunts us.'[34] Later, in 1859, she attended a double bill of *The Porter's Knot* and *Mazeppa*, and remarks: 'There is such a funny song Robson sings, in the last verse of which he speaks of what might have been his lot, had he been a cobbler's son, and sent to the Foundling Hospital, where "the boys are dress'd in woollen clothes to warm their little limbs, and they smell of yellow soap and sing like cherubims".'[35] A visit to the Olympic on 11 March 1861 to see Robson in *The Chimney Corner* was the Queen's penultimate outing to the theatre. Her widowhood and renunciation of all entertainment spared her the pain of witnessing his final appearances, when ebbing self-confidence drove him to drink and death at the age of forty-three.

Both Benjamin Webster, the manager, and Alfred Wigan, who joined the company, were strong reasons for the Queen patronizing the Adelphi, a theatre hitherto characterized more by blood-and-thunder melodrama than royal patrons. While she enjoyed proven pleasures like *Masks and Faces* and *Still Waters Run Deep* in their new surroundings, she found Adelphi melodrama less gentlemanly than that offered by Kean at the Princess's. Thus *The Dead Heart* (a French Revolution story, which its author, Watts Phillips, believed Dickens had read in manuscript and promptly 'borrowed' for *A Tale of Two Cities*) was 'a horrid piece . . . The last scene is the guillotine with poor Robert Landry standing on the scaffold in his shirt. Unfortunately none of the actors were well suited to their parts.'[36]

But if the Adelphi failed to please its royal patron with *The Dead Heart*, it made amends a year later. Dion Boucicault, who had adapted a number of the Princess's melodramas, had parted company from Charles Kean (after marrying his ward and juvenile lead) and made a new name for himself in America, particularly with a series of 'sensation dramas' which gave him opportunities to render 'the pathos of Paddy as acted by Boucicault'. The most successful of these to date was *The Colleen Bawn*, originally staged in New York and produced at the Adelphi in September 1860. The Queen first saw it on 5 February 1861:

An early dinner and went with Albert and the two girls to see the celebrated melodrama in 3 acts by Dion Boucicault, called *Colleen Bawn*, taken from

The Collegians. D. Boucicault and his wife (former Miss Robertson, whom I remember some years ago at the Princess's) acted admirably as the ragged Irish peasant and the Colleen Bawn. The scenery was very pretty, and the whole piece very characteristic and thrilling.

The play at once became a royal choice. Scenes from it were commissioned for the Queen's album. Although the Prince Consort's health had been causing some concern, a return visit was made on 19 February: 'We dined "en famille" and went afterwards with Bertie and Alice etc. to the Adelphi, seeing *The Colleen Bawn* from beginning to end. One could appreciate it more the 2nd time, but my enjoyment was damped by seeing dear Albert so uncomfortable, though he managed to laugh a good deal.'

A third visit was planned for 14 March, but further shadows began to gather. The Duchess of Kent's condition was becoming grave. On the morning in question the Queen 'had a fearful headache which prevented my doing anything, going to lunch or out in the afternoon. It was all from this great anxiety about dearest Mama. Got much better and was able to go with Albert, Alice, and Lenchen, to the Adelphi. Enjoyed seeing *The Colleen Bawn* again, and all the cleverness and wit of it.' It was her last visit to a theatre. Two days later her mother died.

'All the cleverness and wit of it', the final words the Queen wrote about a performance in a theatre, fittingly describe its legacy to her, and her generous appreciation of the theatre and its performers. Legacy it proved to be, for not only did Court mourning for the Duchess rule out further attendance, but before the year was over, her husband was dead at the age of forty-two. Queen Victoria would go to the theatre no more.

6

Theatre Royal

Queen Victoria's love of the theatre in all its forms distinguishes her from the majority of her Hanoverian predecessors, to whom theatre-going was a tedious ritual, not unattended by danger in the form of attempted assassination. It is necessary to trace the royal line back to the House of Stuart to find monarchs as keenly interested in the stage, and two of these (Charles II and James II) had reasons of their own for this concern. The Stuarts were also able and enthusiastic performers in masques, operas, and plays, whereas most of the Hanoverians took no more pleasure in performing than they did in seeing performances. A notable exception to this stricture was Frederick, Prince of Wales (son of George II), who was as fond of the drama as of playing cricket, the latter enthusiasm unhappily leading to his early death from a blow on the head by a cricket ball. In January 1749 he engaged the actor, James Quin, to supervise a performance of *Cato* at Leicester House, in which his son (later George III) played Portius and spoke the Prologue.

Queen Victoria's childhood and upbringing were such as to preclude her participating in family theatricals. But her unflagging interest in the theatre suggests that, had her childhood been freer and happier, she would have relished such a pastime. Her account, given earlier, of the charades at Chatsworth strongly suggests an urge to perform, and her lifelong interest in singing and dancing adds further weight to this belief. Even after her husband's death dancing was one self-indulgence she could not entirely forgo, and at the age of seventy-two she compelled Sir Henry Ponsonby's admiration: 'The Queen danced with Prince Henry; light airy steps in the old courtly fashion; no limp or stick but every figure carefully and prettily danced.'[1] Certainly her own children were actively encouraged to perform, though perhaps more

80

Prince Prince Christian   Duchess of Connaught   Princess Christian   Princess Beatrice
Henry of Battenberg   Duke of Connaught   H.M. The Queen   Grand Duke Sergius   Princess Louise   Princess Victoria of Schleswig Holstein

15 *On previous page*   Ellen Terry and Henry Irving in *Becket*
at Windsor Castle, 1893.
'. . . she is 46 ! !'

16   *Carmen* at Windsor Castle, 1892.
'. . . but oh my dear child, I'm afraid she's really not very nice.'

to educate themselves than to entertain others. Putting on plays was clearly designed as an extension of their French and German classes; Madame Rolande, their French governess, was often *metteur-en-scène* and Prince Albert usually supervised their efforts. There is no record of an English play being performed in his lifetime. The date chosen was generally Twelfth Night or Papa and Mama's wedding anniversary (20 February), or as near as could be arranged. These were family occasions, taking place at Windsor, and there seems no suggestion of any such performances being mounted at Buckingham Palace, although later Osborne and particularly Balmoral were to witness a good deal of home-made entertainment.

Most unexpectedly the favourite choice for these occasions was Racine's *Athalie*, on the face of it a wildly unsuitable text for young performers whose ages ranged from eleven to three. The play had, however, gained a new lease of life as a result of Mendelssohn's incidental music, first heard in 1845 and often performed at Windsor concerts. In 1849 the actor George Bartley was commanded to give a reading of the play at Buckingham Palace, with full orchestral accompaniment, and a specially printed edition of the English text used was published.

Nevertheless it presented huge difficulties for the royal children. The Princess Royal, aged eleven, had to portray the murderous queen, while Princess Alice at eight played both Joad and his wife, one of the most remarkable 'doubles' in stage-history. Their mother proudly copied the programme into her Journal:

Athalie—La Princesse Royale
Josabeth, femme du Grand-Prêtre ⎱
Joad, Grand-Prêtre ⎰ —La Princesse Alice
Agar, servante d'Athalie—La Princesse Hélène
Zacharie, fils de Josabeth—La Princesse Louise
Abner, Officier—Le Prince de Galles
Joas—Le Prince Alfred

La scène est dans le Temple de Jerusalem dans une vestibule de l'appartement du Grand-Prêtre.[2]

This casting throws some doubt on the acting capacity of the Prince of Wales, who would seem more suitable for Joad than his younger sister, but had to be content with the minor part of Abner. The scenery from *Julius Caesar* in which Charles Kean and Macready had competed two years earlier was put to new use, and the company wore specially designed customes 'of fine merino, with gold and silver braid'.[3]

Not surprisingly the text was drastically cut, but the Queen expressed complete satisfaction:

Vicky looked very well and spoke and acted her long and difficult part (the celebrated scene, describing her dream, which is Rachel's great part) really admirably, with immense expression and dignity and with the true French emphasis, which indeed they all did ... Alice was 'méconnaissable' as the Priest, with a white beard and hair. She acted beautifully, Affie very nicely and Bertie very well, but his Roman armour was a little too big for him.[4]

In fact Mama drew him in the offending armour, as well as all the performers in costume. One wonders if the Prince of Wales's interest in uniform, medals, and militaria generally dates from this eposide. Whatever his feelings, his father was delighted: 'My beloved Albert was much pleased, and it came as a complete surprise to him.'

The Royal Family's preoccupation with *Athalie* reached new heights in 1853 when three performances were given between 10 and 13 January in the Tapestry Room. A fuller text was now feasible. 'The whole character of the Tragedy and all the principal scenes could not be well managed last year, for want of actors. A great deal was of course cut out and curtailed to avoid tediousness and to enable the Children to act it',[5] but this time the cast was augmented by offspring from two Court families, the Phipps and the Seymours, and the play ran an hour. Alice was allowed to discard Josabeth, now played by Horatia Seymour, but Bertie had still to content himself with Abner. The Queen thoroughly approved:

Little Horatia acted charmingly, so full of grace and dignity, Alice quite touchingly in the scene where her declamation is accompanied by music and where 'Joad' says 'Pleure, Jerusalem, pleure, cité perfide' ... The 1st part was nearly the same as last year, but the 2nd quite new, and truly beautiful it is. The scene in which Joas is told that he is King and the tableau where he is discovered seated on a throne with a crimson cloak, a crown and sceptre, 2 Levites behind him, and Zacharie and Salaminthe kneeling at his feet, was most effective and very pretty.[6]

By this time Vicky had firmly established herself in the title role and was 'very grand and tragic', carrying off 'the scene of fury, where she rushes out in a rage, extremely well'.[7] But familiarity had perhaps bred contempt. After a successful dress rehearsal and triumphant first night, a further performance was arranged for 13 January, when 'there were divers mishaps. Vicky "à 3 réprises" entirely forgot her part. Little Zacharie (Louise) did not come on when she ought, so that the others had to wait for her. The music, however, was greatly improved by the addition of some other instruments. Alice acted as well, in fact better, than before. Our relations were much pleased.'

Nevertheless *Athalie* was dropped from the repertoire. There had in fact been an offering in a more suitable vein the previous year, when Kotzebue's little pastoral piece, *Das Hahnenschlag* (*The Cockshy*), had been acted on Twelfth Night. Bertie was in his element here as 'Fritz, ein Bauernknabe', and the Queen recorded:

The stage was very prettily arranged and the dresses very nice. There was not a hitch of any kind, and I thought the Children acted very well . . . The Performance commenced with a little Piece from Beethoven's Pastoral Symphony played by Dr Barker behind the scenes. There are 2 little Choruses, the 1st a pretty little German song: 'Arbeit macht das Leben süss', and the concluding pieces from 'La Dame Blanche'. I have made a little sketch.[8]

The whole occasion was evidently as light-hearted as the Queen's sketches of the children in character suggest. Her account concludes: 'The children afterwards danced a little, and then had Snap Dragons' (presumably a Christmas treat).

Das Hahnenschlag was the first of several little German plays put on by the royal children. Less than a month after the accident-hit performance of *Athalie*, they staged *Die Tafelbirnen* (*The Pears*) by Agnes Frantz, 'a charming childish little piece, which the children acted delightfully',[9] overjoyed no doubt to discard the formal Alexandrines and heroic manner of Racine. 'Bertie's nose as "Klaus", the Policeman, at the end of the 1st Act was very droll . . . Nothing could have been prettier or more successful. Vicky in her spectacles was delightful'. Two years later *Red Riding Hood* (teutonically disguised as *Rothkäppchen*) gave Bertie another showy part as 'Ein Wolf', supported by the largest juvenile company yet assembled. Prince Arthur was now old enough to join in, and there were Seymours, Van de Wegens, Greys, and Hoods to swell the ranks.

The performance commenced under difficulties as far as the Queen was concerned. Lord Aberdeen had just submitted the government's resignation, and 'I was a good deal apart afterwards, and could hardly quite pull myself together for the children's pretty little German Play, which took place at a quarter to 6.'[10] Nevertheless 'Alice, with a fair wig and very prettily dressed in red and white, with a little red hat, looked charming, and acted very nicely . . . Bertie did his part of the Wolf particularly well, for it was very difficult.' This time it was Vicky's turn to double 'Margarethe, eine Mühlerin' and 'Die Grossmutter', while Louise, by now seven, gave clear indication of future acting achievement: 'very droll as the whiskered and moustached gentleman, and very pious-looking afterwards as the "Schützgeist" '. Evidently the Queen's preoccupation with politics and politicians was agreeably diverted, and the play was repeated on 20 February, the all-important wedding anniversary.

The first family entertainment of which photographs survive was *Les Deux Petits Savoyards*, performed on 16 January 1854. Vicky had the important role here as 'Madame la Marquise de Verseuil' in whose castle the action takes place, with Bertie as 'Le Bailli', and Affie and Alice as 'Les deux petits Savoyards'. 'It was most successful and was very pretty and our Children did their parts extremely well. Bertie (whom his father had painted to look quite hideous) acted with great spirit, and dear little Lenchen [Princess Helena] was incomparable as Clement, so important, never making a mistake. Everyone was inclined to laugh when she appeared, but she did not perceive it.'[11]

An account from Caley Brothers, the Windsor firm of drapers still in business, discloses that the costumes for *Les Deux Petits Savoyards* cost a total of £45.1s.7½d.[12] The following month Messrs Caley submitted an account for £23.14s.8d. (including £1.5s.6d. for '1 Printed Leopard Skin') in respect of costumes for the *tableaux vivants* performed on 10 February. This was an occasion of some importance, held in the Rubens Room after the professional companies had departed:

The room was entirely darkened. The stage still remained. 5 Tableaux were performed, 4 representing the seasons. *Alice* as *Spring* recited some very pretty verses from Tennyson's Seasons. *Vicky* as *Summer* with dear little Arthur asleep amongst the Cornsheaves also recited verses. *Affie* as Bacchus representing *Autumn* also sang some words. *Bertie* with a long white beard and cloak covered with snow, and *Louise* in a sort of Russian costume, sitting before a Fire, represented *Winter*. He also recited some verses taken and adapted from Thomson's Seasons. The 5th and last one combined the 4 others, which had been separately represented. In the clouds at the back stood dear little Lenchen, reading very pretty verses specially written for the purpose by Mr Martin Tupper, as the Spirit of the Empress Helena.[13]

'The Seasons' inaugurated a tradition of *tableaux vivants* at Court which was to survive the near-fatal blow of Prince Albert's death, and reach full bloom in the last decade of Queen Victoria's reign. Prince Albert himself witnessed two further displays. In February 1856 there was a programme with a strongly Scott (and Scots) flavour: two scenes from *The Lady of the Lake* presented Bertie as James V and Affie as Douglas, with Alice as Mary of Lorraine and Louise as a lady-in-waiting. 'Lenchen' appeared as a falconer and 'looked quite "inconnaissable"' in her beard and blackened eyebrows, which made her look so like dear Papa ... My beloved Albert was much pleased, and the performance was quite a surprise'.[14]

Four years later in St George's Hall a strongly historical sequence was assembled. By this time Vicky was a wife and mother and Bertie had embarked on his forty-year apprenticeship to the throne. The programme was therefore designed for the younger children, notably Arthur and the six-year-old Leopold who appeared as 'The Princes in the Tower'. 'The two little Boys made a beautiful picture. Unfortunately Arthur turned his head away too much.'[15] Nevertheless 'Albert was much pleased', and the picture conjured up is of a happy family gathering less than two years before his death.

For many years after the Queen was widowed her Journal gives scant indication of family theatricals. Crushed as they undoubtedly were by bereavement, it still seems unlikely that the royal children abandoned all attempt at make-believe, but such amusements were best kept from Mama's notice. That some sort of play-making continued is suggested by a momentary gap in the clouds which had gathered over the record of the Queen's private life. At Osborne on 2 January 1865 she noted:

To please the children went down to the Council Room to see the rehearsal of a little Play the Boys are acting, *Box and Cox*. It was a terrible effort, for it reminded me so of many former happy performances, dearest Albert sitting near me, directing everything, and correcting the Children, applauding and encouraging them. Before the Play, Baby made her appearance as a milkmaid, and recited 'Le Pot au Lait'. Arthur looked wonderful in a wig with black eyebrows, also Leopold. Arthur acted exceedingly well.

There is no indication that the Queen saw the performance itself. To these youngest children her permanent mourning must have been especially restrictive. 'Baby' (Princess Beatrice) who was only four when her father died, can have had little recollection of him, and

Leopold, four years older, not much more. It was appropriate, therefore, that the same 'Baby' should ultimately be instrumental in reviving the tradition of plays and *tableaux* in the royal circle.

The death of John Brown in 1883, though received by the Queen with anguish, had an opposite effect on the atmosphere at Court. Brown's dour personality had not merely spread gloom around his sovereign; it had separated her from her children. Beatrice, by this time twenty-five and still unmarried, became her mother's constant companion, and contrary to expectation, their relationship was strengthened by her marriage in 1885 to Prince Henry of Battenberg, who dutifully joined the Queen's household and rapidly gained her heart. The oddly nick-named 'Liko' provided a much needed upsurge of spirits at Court, and the birth of his four children, Alexander ('Drino'), Ena, Leopold, and Maurice, completed this transformation. Queen Victoria's circle became a family again, and one of the many happy consequences was the rebirth of family theatricals.

Influential as Princess Beatrice and her husband were in this process, another figure could claim centre stage. This was Alick Yorke, groom-in-waiting from 1884 and a son of the Earl of Hardwicke. He earned a measure of immortality by being the recipient of the authentic reproof: 'We are not amused.' (He had so tickled a German guest with a *risqué* story that the guest's laughter distracted the Queen, who insisted Yorke repeat the story. The 'We' was not merely Queen Victoria herself but the remainder of the lady guests.) Unlucky on this occasion, Yorke was in general a privileged and much loved member of the Court, not least because of his gifts as an entertainer. He had endeared himself by his comic songs (which included 'The Pigs' and 'Sleepy Song') and monologues, such as 'The Picnic', some years before the Court burst into full theatrical activity. His godson (and great-nephew) Victor Mallet describes him vividly:

He had sparkling eyes, an inquisitive nose, and brown hair neatly brushed and oiled. His figure was short and rotund. He was talkative and witty, and a great amateur actor . . . He dressed in an extravagant manner, with huge buttonholes, jewelled rings and tie-pins. I can remember the whiff of scent that accompanied his entrance into a room.[16]

Mallet also suggests: 'Alick Yorke would from his appearance be described nowadays as an elderly pansy, though he seems to have been the kindest and most virtuous of men, and no breath of scandal ever passed his way.'

For these Court entertainments he could call on a number of useful performers. On the male side Arthur Bigge (later Lord Stamfordham) who became private secretary to the Queen in 1895, having served as assistant to Sir Henry Ponsonby, and the Ponsonby brothers, Arthur and Frederick ('Fritz'), were the star performers. Amongst the ladies pride of place and part went to Ethel Cadogan, a maid of honour from 1880 and a lady of temperament in both senses of the word. Princess Beatrice and Princess Louise also played leading parts from time to time. Princess Louise had married the Marquis of Lorne in 1871, but the marriage had proved childless and unhappy, and after her husband's term of office as Governor-General of Canada finished in 1883 she was granted a residence on the Osborne estate, close to that of her sister and Prince Henry. Princess Louise had real artistic gifts and found consolation in exercising them.

Indeed the series of royal theatricals may be said to be therapeutic in origin. The Empress Frederick's daughter, another Vicky, had been invited to England in 1889 to get over her unhappy love affair with Prince Alexander of Battenberg, 'Liko's' brother, which had been crushed by diplomatic obstructions. At Balmoral doing a play was prescribed as a pick-me-up, and Ethel Cadogan put together a three-hander with the inauspicious title, *Caught at Last*. Nevertheless the piece was a big success:

After dinner, Vicky, Mr Yorke, and Ethel C. acted a little most ridiculous piece called *Caught at Last*. Vicky and Mr Yorke did the chief parts and Ethel only a small maid's part. They did it so well. We were kept in fits of laughter. The piece is translated from the French. The performance was at the end of the Drawing room, opening into the Ball Room. There was no real stage, just a curtain, and flowers to mark off the end of the room. Besides the Ladies and Gentlemen, a few of the servants were present.[17]

There was a repeat performance next day, which 'went even better. Vicky has a decided turn for acting and Mr Yorke was inimitable, as he always is. As the little piece only took half an hour, Mr Yorke afterwards gave his most killingly funny "Picnic" which I had not heard again for 7 or 8 years, and which was as clever as ever'.[18] On 28 June the performance was given again for Beatrice's benefit in the White Drawing-Room at Windsor, and afterwards Alick Yorke sang three comic songs in costume. Later that year Ethel's effort achieved a professional performance at the Avenue Theatre, London.

Caught at Last inaugurated a succession of about a dozen Court

87

plays by courtier players. Some members of the Royal Family were less than enthusiastic about participating, and Prince 'Eddie', Duke of Clarence, wrote of 'these tiresome theatricals' at Osborne in February 1891.[19] The pieces chosen were predictably short and slight. Only one (*She Stoops to Conquer*) could be called a classic, and two more (*Used Up* and *A Scrap of Paper*) might just qualify as full-length. The greater number were farces, generally of thirty or more years earlier (*Popping the Question, Cool as a Cucumber, Poor Pillicoddy*). It is relevant to note that these farces were the Queen's favourites, both on her visits to the theatre and at the Windsor Command Performances, rather than dramatic masterpieces, tragic or comic. Somehow one feels that had she not been Queen, or had she married a husband with less highbrow tastes, they were the plays she would have enjoyed acting herself.

Certainly she exercised a lively control over their performance. She attended rehearsals, made suggestions as to 'business', and revised the script as necessary. In *She Stoops to Conquer* at Osborne in January 1893 Princess Louise played Kate Hardcastle and Princess Beatrice was Constance Neville. Fritz Ponsonby as Marlow received a royal rebuke for overdoing his familiarity with Kate as the barmaid, followed next day by another for underplaying the part.[20] In *Used Up* at Balmoral in October 1889 Princess Beatrice was cast as Mrs Ironbrace, a part which disappears from the play after Act I. The Queen decided that the script must be rewritten, and Arthur Bigge suggested a programme note: 'The return and reconciliation of Mrs Ironbrace is by command!' She also made cuts in this play, as Bigge records: 'The result of the rehearsal is that H.M. thinks I had better not call her daughter "a degraded woman" and I agree! Also she is not to say to Sir C. in describing her wooing of Clutterbuck "I have nothing to offer as my dowry but my virtue," to which C. replies, "Ah, little enough." '[21]

The great majority of the performances were at Balmoral, where the Court made extended stays and which clearly lacked indoor diversions. Albani, the Covent Garden soprano, who had a summer retreat nearby at Old Mar Lodge, was regularly called on to sing, and in 1890 George Grossmith brought his own piano and his imitation of 'Mr Henry Irving and his little Dog'. Perhaps the most nerve-racking occasion for the performers was the production on 24 October 1893 of *A Scrap of Paper*. Not only was it a full-length piece with serious moments outside the cast's normal range, but the audience included Sir Henry Campbell-Bannerman, then Secretary for War, Squire Bancroft, and Forbes-Robertson, with other members of the company who were due to perform *Diplomacy* on the same stage two days later. The royal amateurs do not appear to have been overawed by the professionals out front, for the Queen noted loyally: 'The 1st Act of the Play is beyond anything funny, and the whole most amusing',[22] and insisted on a repeat performance next day, when 'It was again excellent and there was not a hitch.'[23] Difficult in rehearsals as Queen Victoria might be, she was a model spectator. Scarcely a performance is noted without a concluding 'We were all in fits of laughter', and after *Caught at Last* young Vicky wrote proudly to her mother: 'No one enjoyed it more than the Queen. I heard her laugh heartily many a time during the piece.'[24] Any performer will recognize the value of such a member of the audience, particularly if that member has sat in on rehearsals and grown familiar with the jokes.

There is no indication that Prince Henry of Battenberg appeared in the plays. On the contrary there is some evidence that his English and his general manner would have been more of a liability than an asset. Marie Mallet had no sooner joined the Court at Osborne as maid-of-honour than

I was summoned to warble duets with Prince Henry, fearfully difficult selections from Gounod's operas, which *he* knew *perfectly well*, and which I was expected to sing at sight. I enacted the role of Juliet, Mireille, and I do not know what else while he shouted violent sentiments such as 'ange adorable!' at me and at one moment it was so comic that I nearly laughed outright; he has a good voice but cannot manage it and sings with very little expression. Princess Beatrice accompanied and smiled benignly.[25]

Nevertheless so sociable and convivial a man was anxious to join in the theatricals, and one may attribute a good deal of the momentum behind the *tableaux vivants* to him and to his wife's sympathetic attitude. These in fact antedate the plays by over a year. At Osborne on Twelfth Night, 1888, a programme of four *tableaux* was staged, with Princess Beatrice as Queen Elizabeth to her husband's Raleigh, and the Queen of Sheba to a decidedly grizzled Solomon in Sir Henry Ponsonby. Prince Henry also appeared as a Toreador in a *Carmen* scene, with Marie Mallet as a dancing girl in what she claimed were 'very short petti-coats',[26] though the photographs scarcely support her.

The most interesting item was the last, 'Homage to Queen Victoria'. The stage erected was unusually elaborate—it had been assembled for the Kendals' performance the previous February—and full use was made of its pictorial scope for the finale:

... Beatrice, Liko, and the others sat with us to see the last Tableau, 'Homage', which was a very unexpected surprise! My bust being wreathed with flowers stood in the centre and the ladies were grouped round behind it. The Band played 'Home, sweet Home'. This brought to a close what really were lovely Tableaux and a great treat.[27]

A similar, though even more elaborate, compliment was paid to 'Liko' at Balmoral that autumn. His birthday fell on 5 October, and a series of *tableaux* was prepared, the initial letter of each scene spelling out the names 'Henry Maurice', i.e.

Harvest
Elizabeth (Beatrice as the Saint, not Queen on this occasion)
Novice
Rebecca
York (the Princes in the Tower once more)
Malcolm Canmore
Antigone
Union (marital—a Hessian peasant wedding)
Romeo
India (Beatrice 'wearing quantities of my Indian jewellery')
Charles Edward (the Young Pretender)
Elsa[28]

So ambitious was this performance that it had to be spread over two days, 'Maurice' being performed on 6 October. Some of the casting now seems to have an almost tragic insight: for example 'Eddie' (the Duke of Clarence) portrayed the Young Pretender, one heir who never inherited representing another; and in 'Novice', a convent scene, the central figure was 'Alicky', Princess Alice's youngest child, then only sixteen, whose fate as the Czarina Alexandra owed so much to her religious devotion. Less tragic figures were the Juliet (Bertie's daughter, Maud, later to be Queen of Norway), and her sister 'Louise of Wales', as the bride in 'Union'. Beatrice, besides appearing as Saint Elizabeth and Mother India, portrayed Queen Margaret in 'Malcolm Canmore', and 'Liko' Canmore himself and Telramund in 'Elsa'.

On the whole the plays put on at Court used only the simplest scenery and contemporary dress. An exception to this was *She Stoops to Conquer*, for which the services of Willie Clarkson, London's leading wigmaker and costumier, were employed. He relates that when after the performance he was summoned to receive the Queen's appreciation, she burst out laughing, and looking down, he saw that he had omitted to remove the carpet slippers in which he preferred to work.[29] His solecism was forgiven and his costumes used for most of the *tableaux*, generally chosen for their decorative potential. Royalties of history were understandably popular: Mary Queen of Scots at Fotheringhay was portrayed by Princess Louise at Osborne in January 1890 ('Her expression was beautiful and sad beyond measure' wrote the Queen)[30] and in the same programme Louise appeared as Queen Philippa in 'The Surrender of Calais'; 'Eddie' appeared as King Duncan in a *Macbeth* scene at Balmoral that year, and King Richard and Queen Berengaria figured a year later, with the Marquis of Lorne as King Richard, and his sister-in-law, not his wife, as Berengaria. Queen Louise of Prussia 'after Richter' was represented in the same programme by Arthur's wife, the Duchess of Connaught, and later 'King Arthur and his Court' very properly featured the Duke of Connaught in the name-part with 'Liko' as Sir Lancelot. An Oriental scene was always popular. Not only did Princess Beatrice personify Mother India; there was a 'Bedouin Encampment' at Osborne in January 1890; an 'Arab Encampment' and 'Oriental Bazaar' ('Abdul had helped to arrange it')[31] at Balmoral the same year; 'The Snake Charmer' in June 1893, and 'An Indian Scene' a year later. Such dispositions may be interpreted as a sop to the unpopular Munshi, Abdul Karim, and his numerous friends and relations all anxious to be in on the proceedings. When Beatrice portrayed the Indian Empire, 'all my Indian people helped to form the group. One of the servants made a salaam in front of Beatrice, presenting a gold plate to her.'[32] This was artistically defensible, but the previous day the Munshi and two of his cronies, Mahomed and Ahmed, had somehow squeezed themselves into 'Rebecca, taken from Horace Vernet's picture'.

The *tableaux vivants* at Windsor more than thirty years earlier had been a chance for the children to show off. The later series were mostly adult affairs, though occasionally the younger generation was admitted, and 'Liko' and his son Alexander ('Drino') portrayed Hubert and Arthur in a *King John* scene at Balmoral on 24 May 1894 ('My poor old 75th birthday'), and the previous year 'Baby B' (daughter of the Duke of Edinburgh) 'appeared as a portrait in a large hat, in the days of Charles I' for a *Sleeping Beauty* episode.[33] On the Queen's birthday that year the children were encouraged to present a *tableaux* programme of their own:

The subjects were: Little Red Ridinghood, Jack and Jill, Cinderella, Mother

Hubbard's Tale and Grandmama's Birthday. Grandmama's Birthday almost brought tears to my eyes. Sandra [another of the Edinburgh daughters] looked so nice with a grey wig, wearing one of my caps, and Leopold in her arms. The whole was so prettily arranged and gave me great pleasure.[34]

At Osborne in 1891 the whole Connaught family appeared in a Japanese scene: 'The Children were quite charming in their Japanese dresses; Patsy [later Lady Patricia Ramsay] with an enormous bow on her back and a fan was too delightful.'[35]

The elaborate staging of these programmes, which lasted anything from an hour to two hours, called for careful stage-management. 'Each had 2 poses, and each pose was shown 3 times'[36] writes the Queen of the *tableaux* in the 'Henry Maurice' programme, and this seems to have been a regular convention. Clearly a proscenium-arch and efficient drop-curtain were essential, if not always something as impressive as that left behind at Osborne by the Kendals. Music was vital, both for the *tableaux* themselves and during the intervals, which must have been extensive, in view of the numerous scenic and costume changes required. At Osborne the Band of the Royal Marine Light Infantry could be summoned across the Solent from Portsmouth, and at Balmoral a professional orchestra under Mr Curtis was usually available, although on at least one occasion the versatile Beatrice 'sang and played on the Harmonium'.[37] The Queen, appreciative and even indulgent where acting was concerned, applied sterner standards to the orchestra. 'The performance was a wonderful success, excepting the music, which was perfectly disgraceful',[38] was her judgment on *Used Up*. Skilled control of lighting must also have been necessary, particularly in view of the inflexibility of gas-jets and battens. Balmoral, which had no mains supply of gas but relied on kerosene lamps, presented particular problems. On one occasion the Queen recorded: 'The lighting was not quite successful'[39] but otherwise the stage-staff acquitted themselves admirably.

It is tempting to speculate on the appeal of these *tableaux*. For the performers they had all the novelty of dressing-up and showing off without the tedium of endless rehearsals and line-learning. For the spectator in the pre-cinema age they offered pictorial satisfaction, even a minimum of movement (hence the '2 poses'). They were also free of the taint which fully-fledged theatrical performances still carried in some circles, and which even inhibited so ardent a theatre-lover as Queen Victoria from entering a playhouse after her widow-

hood. But there seems to have been another element in their popularity
—a desire, before the universal availability of cameras and amateur
photography, to fix a moment of historical or geographical interest
on the mind's eye. The commonest form of home-made entertainment
today must be 'showing our holiday snaps'. For some late Victorians
it was the *tableau vivant*.

In 1895 after ten years as a surrogate-son rather than a son-in-law,
'Liko's' patience was exhausted. The outbreak of the Ashanti War on
the Gold Coast had fired his ambition. Instead of portraying Sir
Walter Raleigh or Sir Lancelot in *tableaux vivants* he longed to prove
himself a true knight in action. The Queen was persuaded to release him
and he sailed for West Africa. Within weeks he fell victim to the
dreaded typhus fever. He was ordered home, but at Madeira on the
return journey he died. He was thirty-seven. With Beatrice a widow
and her children fatherless, the spirit of family theatricals was ex-
tinguished. The Queen still witnessed the occasional Command
Performance; as late as 1899 she summoned 'Lord' George Sanger's
Circus to give a display in Windsor Castle grounds, and teased the
proprietor about his self-service title.[40] But there were no more plays,
and no more *tableaux vivants*. No one had the heart for them.

7

The Queen Commands

Two grievous losses—that of her mother in March 1861, followed by her husband in December—brought Queen Victoria's theatregoing to an abrupt and irrevocable close. Even the strict conventions of her age did not demand such immense sacrifices of a widow. The impressive record of her theatregoing over the preceding thirty years suggests that her withdrawal from the theatre was a deliberate act of abstinence, especially as she allowed herself in later years to attend the occasional public concert. When it is remembered that the Queen was only forty-two at her husband's death and that she survived him by nearly forty years, the depth of her feeling is movingly demonstrated.

To take only one example of this self-denial: the Queen admired and actively furthered the career of Arthur Sullivan, the leading English composer of the period (and this encouragement makes a striking contrast with the lukewarm attitude she adopted during her husband's lifetime towards such native musicians as Michael Balfe and Vincent Wallace). But although she often sang excerpts from the Savoy Operas for her private pleasure, she never allowed herself to see them at the Savoy, and the two D'Oyly Carte performances given before her at Windsor and Balmoral in 1891 coincided with the last successful year of Gilbert and Sullivan's partnership. Even more striking is her failure to see *Ivanhoe*, the 'grand' opera she had urged Sullivan to write, and which he dedicated to her.

That the Queen was human and sometimes hungered for the fruit she had forbidden herself is clear from a letter she wrote to Sir Henry Ponsonby in 1892, regarding an exhibition at which the delights of Venice were reconstructed in three dimensions:

Does Sir Henry Ponsonby think it possible for her to go *privately* to see *Venice*? She hears it is really admirably done. Princess Beatrice is delighted and it is a real success. In the day of course and it is not a theatre or a play and it will be 5 months and a half after her dear grandson's death and 3 and a half after her dear son-in-law's and she would very much like to see it.[1]

Her private secretary strongly urged her to go. But the theatre was a different matter, and the Queen would not consider breaking her rule. Instead the theatre had to come to her.

The years between 1861 and 1887, when the Queen started to command performances again, marked a period of steadily increasing respectability and refinement in the English theatre. To this movement the encouragement shown by the Windsor performances and the Royal Family's sustained patronage of English plays and players in the 1850s contributed greatly. It is possible to trace the development of many features of the revival of the '50s into the '60s and '70s, when early promise turned in most, though not all, respects to fully-fledged performance. The achievements of Charles Kean at the Princess's, for example, with his blend of spectacular Shakespeare and 'gentle-manly melodrama', were built on by Irving at the Lyceum, where his repertoire consisted of precisely these two elements, many of the melodramas being Kean's own vehicles. The major difference was that Charles and Ellen Kean were honest craftsmen, whereas in Irving and Ellen Terry the Lyceum possessed two leading players of magnetic personality. The decidedly tentative efforts of managers like Webster and Wigan to foster a native school of comedy, which in their hands aspired no higher than *Masks and Faces* or *Still Waters Run Deep*, found subtler exponents in Squire and Marie Bancroft and their company, and a writer with a more delicate touch in Tom Robertson. The extravaganzas mounted by Vestris and Mathews at the Lyceum and the singular strain of originality in burlesque achieved by Robson at the Olympic were recognized by Richard D'Oyly Carte as a vein he could profitably trust W. S. Gilbert and Arthur Sullivan to mine, and the Savoy Operas and the Savoy Theatre itself were impressive proofs of his insight.

All these enterprises would have faltered and failed without support from an increasingly intelligent and discriminating public, and to such a public the Queen in her seclusion from society no longer gave a lead. One may speculate what would have been the fate of Irving's National Theatre in embryo, or Tom Robertson's diminutive dramas, if her marriage had proved childless or if her family had ignored the theatre and its sister arts as completely as some of the earlier Hanoverians. In the event most of the Queen's children then old enough took a lively interest in the arts during her seclusion. The Duke of Edinburgh, for example, was devoted to music, and though his friends found his violin-playing more penance than pleasure, he used his influence well and widely. Princess Louise was another member of the Royal Family interested and accomplished in the arts, and who, since (unlike her elder sisters) she married a native of Great Britain, had more opportunity than they to pursue that interest.

The key-figure in this situation, however, was the Queen's heir, and though such modest evidence as exists suggests that the Prince of Wales had not inherited artistic gifts, there is no question of his ready and invaluable encouragement of the theatre during his 'apprenticeship'. From 1863, moreover, his patronage of the arts was greatly enhanced by the presence of the Princess of Wales beside him, and together they were increasingly seen at important theatrical occasions, including many first nights. Irving in particular was regularly supported by the royal couple, even before he became manager as well as star of the Lyceum. When they attended *Charles I* there in 1872, the audience treated W. G. Wills's lumbering verse-play as a blood-and-thunder melodrama, cheering the Royalists and hissing the Puritans like the deepest-dyed of villains.[2] The Prince's dramatic taste may not have been overnice: he is reputed to have said of Irving's first *Hamlet* (1875) that 'the only thing worth looking at was Isabel Bateman's [the Ophelia] face'.[3] His great contribution to Irving's enterprise, however, was to be seen increasingly on the make-or-break occasions; he attended the first nights of *Romeo and Juliet* (1882) and *Faust* (1885), when he went backstage and held up the scene-changes.[4] He also graced a number of social and charitable functions at the Lyceum, for example the supper on stage to mark the triumphant run of *Much Ado About Nothing* (May 1883) and a matinée the following month to raise funds for the Royal College of Music, at which Irving and his much-loved fellow artiste, J. L. Toole, played Robert Macaire and Jacques Strop.[5] By 1890 he was attending the theatre sixty-seven times in one year.[6]

Not all the Prince's associations with the theatre were so auspicious. On 1 March 1870, a week after being subpoenaed to give evidence in the notorious Mordaunt divorce-case, he was loudly booed at the Olympic, despite the presence of the Princess of Wales beside him.[7]

17 and 18 *Tableaux Vivants* at Balmoral, 1888.
(above) 'The Novice' portrayed by the future Tsarina Alexandra.
(below) 'Charles Edward, the Young Pretender' portrayed by
Prince 'Eddy', Duke of Clarence.

19 *Tableaux Vivants* at Osborne, 1888.
'Homage to Queen Victoria.'

His interest in such diverse artistes as Hortense Schneider and Sarah Bernhardt was also the subject of a good deal of comment. Worthier of serious consideration is the Prince's part in furthering the theatrical career of Lillie Langtry. In 1881, four years after she had first caught his eye, the 'Jersey Lily' decided to go on the stage in a desperate bid to recoup her finances. The Prince attended the special charity matinée at the Haymarket when Mrs Langtry played Kate in *She Stoops to Conquer* with a professional cast, and the success of this début led to her engagement by the Bancrofts for the part of Blanche Haye in their revival of Robertson's Crimean War comedy, *Ours*. There is some indication that her royal admirer attended rehearsals and helped to coach the lady, although he did not go to the first night on 19 January 1882; he certainly saw the piece three times during the first month of its run which, though brief, gave the necessary impetus to Mrs Langtry's career.[8]

It may be asked: was Mrs Langtry a capable actress, or was her subsequent profitable career in the theatre on both sides of the Atlantic over twenty years based purely on her beauty and of course her reputation as a princely favourite? That audiences initially crowded to see her because of her fame is clear enough. On the other hand she was chiefly trained for the stage by Henrietta Hodson, an exacting taskmistress (with whom she shortly quarrelled); the Bancrofts were far too fastidious to cast her in a leading role if her performance as Kate had indicated she possessed beauty without talent; and although she was in subsequent years usually her own manageress, she was also engaged for the Criterion by so shrewd an actor-manager as Charles Wyndham. Certain of her performances, including Shakespeare's Cleopatra (a role in which professional beauties mostly fail) were widely praised. Although lacking the discipline of the great actress, Mrs Langtry, it seems sufficiently proven, could act.

One important occasion on which the Prince of Wales showed how fully the Court now recognized the new status of the acting profession also derived at least in part from his personal concern for Mrs Langtry's career. This was the dinner he gave at Marlborough House on 19 February 1882 (during the run of *Ours* at the Haymarket). There were thirty-seven guests in all, and a number of these came from the theatre, including Irving, Bancroft, Wyndham, Hare, Kendal, and Grossmith amongst the performers, and Burnand and Sala amongst the writers. There were also a number of titled guests, one of whom, Lord Carrington, wrote afterwards to his wife that the stage-folk were sandwiched between ordinary mortals with more or less success. I sat next to Kendal, a good-looking bounder, who distinguished himself later in the evening by singing a very vulgar song which was not favourably received in high quarters ... Irving and Bancroft were the great guns ... but it was a dullish evening.[9]

The vulgar song sounds a highly uncharacteristic lapse by Kendal, whose wife (later Dame Madge) sported the straightest laces in the profession. In any case it did not harm Kendal's career or change the Prince's benevolent attitude towards his calling.

Four months before the Marlborough House dinner, the Prince had been successful in persuading his mother to witness her first performance for over twenty years. The author of the play in question, F. C. Burnand, was present at that dinner, though probably more in his capacity as editor of *Punch*; and the event took place at Abergeldie Castle, within driving distance of Balmoral, which since his marriage the Prince had made his home during the grouse-shooting season.

The performance was given by Mr Edgar Bruce's Company. Bruce, who by a coincidence had a lease of the Prince of Wales's Theatre in London, was a worthy but by no means leading actor-manager. He had, however, achieved a remarkable success the previous spring with *The Colonel*, Burnand's amiable jest at the expense of the Aesthetic Movement, in which Beerbohm Tree, a young actor just gaining recognition, played Lambert Streyke, a recognizable portrait of Oscar Wilde. Both the actor's and the play's success may have confirmed an enormously popular librettist in his decision to change a scenario about a clerical idol called the Reverend Lawn Tennison[10] into a comic opera about a poet called Bunthorne, for *Patience* was first produced at the Opera Comique two months after *The Colonel* had opened.

The success of Burnand's piece also encouraged Bruce to set up a touring company of *The Colonel*, while the original cast played on profitably at the Prince of Wales's. In the touring version Bruce himself appeared as Colonel Wootteweell W. Wood, US Cavalry, and William Hawtrey drooped divertingly as Lambert Streyke. By late September the tour had reached the Theatre Royal, Edinburgh, where the company opened on Monday 24 September. But the preceding Sunday Bruce had been summoned to Abergeldie Castle, where

He at once grasped the situation, and seeing that the huge coachhouses of the Castle were capable of being converted into a charming miniature Theatre, he with the consent of Mr Howard, the Manager of the Theatre Royal, Edinburgh, secured the assistance of Mr Fred Dangerfield, the scenic artist, and Mr Smith, the stage-carpenter of that establishment, and was enabled to give in miniature an exact reconstruction of those scenes now in use at the Prince of Wales's Theatre, London.[11]

Even before the curtain fell on the last performance at Edinburgh that Saturday, the theatre's scenic artist and carpenter were busy at Abergeldie. The company travelled by train on the Monday, and proceeded to the castle next day. The performance which followed engagingly combined extremes of occasion and entertainment. Burnand's modest joke in a makeshift setting must have struck the mildest of notes, as the *Era* report seems aware: 'Notwithstanding the cramped dimensions of the stage and still more trying ordeal of performing before such an unusually brilliant audience, every point was made and the "Colonel's" well-known lines about the egg literally convulsed the entire audience with laughter.'[12]

On the other hand the Queen's patronage of a play for the first time in more than twenty years, together with the presence of the Prince and Princess of Wales, as well as Princesses Louise and Beatrice, called for ceremonial of some kind, which was not lacking:

The scene presented was a most charming and unusual one, the gillies, with lighted torches and the pipers surrounding a brilliant assemblage of the nobility and beauty of the Court. A gigantic bonfire at the entrance to the Theatre illuminated the surrounding hills, and added to the grandeur of the spectacle.[13]

Well-known lines about the egg fall oddly against spectacular grandeur, but the spectator for whom all this was devised responded warmly, almost as though she had been attending plays no less regularly for the past twenty years as during the thirty years which preceded her withdrawal from the theatre:

Dined at 8, and after wishing poor Leopold good night, who was much disappointed at being prevented from going with us—all went to Abergeldie, where a theatrical performance was given at the coachhouse. At the end of it a small stage was erected, and beautifully arranged with plants and flowers. Bertie and Alix received us at the door. The room was very full, Bertie having invited the servants and tenants . . . The piece given was *The Colonel* in 3 acts, a very clever play, written to quiz and ridicule the foolish aesthetic people who dress in such an absurd manner, with loose garments, large puffed sleeves, great hats, and carrying peacock's feathers, sun-flowers and lilies. It was very well acted, and strange to say, most of the actors are gentlemen by birth, who have taken to the stage as a profession . . . It was the first time I had seen professionals act a regular play since March '61. Mr Bruce presented me with a nosegay and playbill before we went in, and I spoke to him at the conclusion of the performance. We got home shortly before 12, having been very much amused.[14]

Perhaps the most significant comment the Queen makes in this account is 'strange to say, most of the actors are gentlemen by birth, who have taken to the stage as a profession'. Thirty year earlier she had commented on the exceptional gentility of a Charles James Mathews or Alfred Wigan. Now it is the rule rather than the exception she notices. She was careful to record that 'Mr Hawtrey is the son of Mr Hawtrey who has little Eton', i.e. of the Rev Hawtrey (himself the cousin of a Provost of Eton) who was head of the preparatory school. Charles Kean had been educated briefly at Eton. Now Old Etonians were competing for the theatrical profession, and in fact a younger brother, Charles Hawtrey, made his début in the London production of *The Colonel* in the same month that William appeared before the Queen at Abergeldie.

Edgar Bruce's Company had a number of reasons for remembering the occasion. After the Queen drove back to Balmoral, the Prince of Wales gave them supper, which lasted until 2 a.m. They were then taken to their hotel at Ballater, for the briefest of nights, since they caught a special train from Ballater Station at 7 a.m. This brought them to Carlisle at six that evening, and they were on stage at Her Majesty's Theatre by eight.[15] Certainly the life of a touring actor, even those who had just played before a Crowned Head, was exacting.

The Abergeldie performance did not, as might have been expected, lead to a series of Command Performances, still less to the Queen's resumption of theatregoing. In fact she did not see another play for over five years. That her son tried to organize a 'return engagement' seems clear from correspondence between Sir Dighton Probyn, the Prince's secretary, and Henry Irving in 1889, about the proposed performance of *The Bells* and the trial scene from *The Merchant of Venice* at Sandringham, which mentions *en passant*: 'You will remember that some years ago when the Queen was coming here, but prevented by an accident from doing so, that you then were coming down to act before Her Majesty . . .'[16] But was it only 'an accident' that prevented another Command Performance for five and a half years? After all, John Brown stood at the Queen's side until 1883, and seems unlikely to have favoured such frivolities. The inauguration of a series of performances at Court with the Kendals' visit to Osborne in 1887 was, like the amateur theatricals and *tableaux vivants*, a celebration of the new family atmosphere consequent upon Princess Beatrice's marriage.

Over the curious episode of *The Colonel* at Abergeldie there hovers the whimsical spirit of Oscar Wilde and the Aesthetic Movement. It was surely their notoriety, not the modest merits of Burnand's little joke or Bruce's 2nd XI, that rightly convinced the Prince of Wales his mother could be tempted to bend (though not break) her rule of twenty years' standing. Perhaps 'Mr Hawtrey, son of Mr Hawtrey who has Little Eton' would have been justified that night in interpolating into his part as Lambert Streyke some lines by the much admired Fleshly Poet, Reginald Bunthorne:

> And every one will say,
> As you walk your flowery way,
> 'If he's content with a vegetable love which would
> certainly not suit *me*,
> Why, what a most particularly pure young man this pure
> young man must be!'

It would be pleasing to think that the invitation to Mr and Mrs Kendal to stage a double bill of *Uncle's Will* and *Sweethearts* at Osborne on 1 February 1887 was conceived as an opening to Golden Jubilee year, but the timing seems more coincidence than commemoration. At any rate the performance bore more plentiful fruit than that of *The Colonel*. In the next twelve years the Queen saw twenty-one performances, widely varied in content but all affording her considerable pleasure. The Osborne performance itself was something of an experiment—there were inadequate facilities for large-scale productions —and on her next outing, to see Irving and Ellen Terry at Sandringham, the Queen was a guest. But the remaining twenty performances were divided between Windsor and Balmoral, and chosen by her. Certain factors besides the Queen's own taste affected the division of performances—at Windsor ten out of the fourteen programmes were opera, at Balmoral three were plays and three operetta. At Windsor (with one exception) the performances were given in the Waterloo Chamber—a much more sympathetic venue than either the Rubens

Room or St George's Hall, and one in which music and drama (including plays by the Royal Shakespeare Company) have been heard in recent years. St George's Hall was used for dressing-rooms. Gordon Craig, who played the Third Templar—'I had three lines to speak—that was, I think, in the second act'—in Irving's production of *Becket* at Windsor in 1893—describes the atmosphere backstage:

Each cubicle, as it were—each screened-off dressing-room—had above it, on the high wall, a very tall portrait of a king, queen or princess, from far back down to modern times. About 130 feet—would that be the length of the gallery? I don't know, but it was very long. And this chatter went on, and strange lights shot up and dispersed, from the candles or lamps or whatever we had to make-up by.

Soon we heard an abrupt voice at the far end of the passage, and that meant the coming of the Queen was being announced. So the conversation died away completely—though every now and then you would hear someone mutter 'got a spot of spirit gum?' 'Hush!' And then quiet—not even a shuffle of feet. Evidently the Queen was passing through the gallery at the other end and taking her seat in the hall.[17]

The size of the Waterloo Chamber scarcely favoured intimate drama. After a couple of experiments—John Hare in *A Pair of Spectacles* and *A Quiet Rubber*, and the Comédie Française—it was clearly thought desirable to use the facilities for something bigger. *Becket* was in fact the only other play staged there—a pageant-drama of operatic proportions. When Duse was invited to perform *La Locandiera* at Windsor in 1894, she and her company were assigned to the White Drawing-Room.

At Balmoral the performances were given in the Ballroom, a setting suitable for plays but somewhat cramped for operetta. The main restriction here, however, was one of available companies. Only those already touring in the north could be invited, and the summer and early autumn were somewhat lean seasons in this respect. The D'Oyly Carte 'C' Company were playing at Her Majesty's, Aberdeen, in September 1891, and cancelled a performance there to give *The Mikado* at Balmoral.[18] Hare's revival of *Diplomacy* finished a tour at Glasgow in October 1893, and thus the company were able to accede to the royal command. Tree's Company from the Haymarket played *The Ballad Monger* and *The Red Lamp* in 1894, then travelled to Holyhead and embarked for Dublin, where they appeared the night after their Command Performance, having survived a peculiarly

Irish Sea which prevented their docking until a quarter of an hour before the curtain rose.[19]

Despite the long break, the Queen's recollection of her playgoing days was clear and cherished. When Mrs Kendal was presented after the Osborne performance, the Queen talked to her of some of the earlier actors she had seen, such as Macready, the Charles Keans, Charles James Mathews, Wigan, and the Keeleys.[20] After the excerpt from *The Merchant of Venice* at Sandringham, she recorded: 'Irving played the part of Shylock extremely well,—Miss Ellen Terry that of Portia beautifully. I often saw her sister Kate formerly, and as a child in the part of Prince Arthur at Windsor.'[21] She had of course seen Miss Ellen Terry herself as Puck and Mamillius, but *King John* was always a treasured memory. In *Diplomacy* at Balmoral the heroine was played by Kate Rorke, and after the performance 'I spoke to her about her old aunt, the celebrated Miss Woolgar, whom I had seen so often in former days'.[22] This was a generous gesture since the celebrated Miss Woolgar was by no means one of the Queen's favourites. *The School for Scandal*, at Windsor in 1857 'was extremely well acted, with the exception of the part of "Lady Teazle" which Miss Woolgar (Mrs Mellon) spoilt'.[23] Even more generous was the Queen's request to the Kendals that they include in their company for Osborne Rowley Cathcart, whom she remembered acting with the Keans thirty years earlier,[24] since Rowley Cathcart was a far from distinguished or prominent member of the Princess's Company, where he was over-shadowed by his elder brother, James Cathcart, one of Kean's trusted lieutenants.

While the Queen was consistently appreciative of the acting offered her, she was chiefly impressed by the gentility of the actors, of which the Edgar Bruce Company had already given her a taste. Her account of the Sandringham performance concludes: 'I waited a moment in the Drawing room to speak to Irving and Ellen Terry. He is very gentle-man-like, and she very pleasing and handsome.'[25] After *A Pair of Spectacles* she found 'Mr Hare is a very small, spare, gentlemanlike man, and is a gentleman, as so many are nowadays.'[26] The last English play she saw was *Liberty Hall* by the St James's Company in 1895, which 'was very well acted by Mr George Alexander and his company. He is an excellent actor, a gentleman, and his real name is Mason.'[27] Her hearing was beginning to fail her—Alexander's real name was Sansom—but her instinct was still sound.

This performance was particularly well documented by a member of the company, S. Kinsey Peile, another gentleman, in fact a retired Army officer, who earlier that year had had the distinction of creating the small but effective part of Lane, the manservant, in *The Importance of Being Earnest*, and thus begun the first performance of the most celebrated play to be written in Queen Victoria's reign. After the events at the Old Bailey in April and May of 1895 it was unthinkable that the Queen should be exposed to that trivial comedy for serious people, and *Liberty Hall*, R. C. Carton's equally trivial comedy in a Robertsonian vein, was an innocuous alternative. Nearly thirty years later Peile included an account of the visit to Balmoral, no doubt embellished by repetition, in his autobiography.[28] The St James's Company seem to have behaved with an abandon unexpected from so dignified an establishment. No sooner had they arrived than their leading lady, Evelyn Millard, spying a pram escorted by two nurse-maids and two plainclothes policemen, rushed over, exclaiming 'Oh look! a baby!', only to be rebuffed by the equerry in charge of their group with the words: 'Come back, please; do not approach the Royal infant' (in fact the future Edward VIII). For the performance the Queen was carried in a chair to the door of the Ballroom, and Peile defied etiquette to peep at her from the dressing-room. The Ballroom itself was a battlefield of scents; the smell of kerosene lamps being countered by perfume poured into red-hot shovels, waved by foot-men. 'There was no applause until Her Majesty applauded, no laughter until Her Majesty laughed, which gave a strange air of unreality to the performance', although he admits 'Her Majesty having applauded and laughed frequently', the evening 'had gone exceedingly well'.[29]

One small detail in his account movingly links the performance to the Queen's earlier playgoing. Amongst the company was E. M. Robson, a relation of the little comedian she had so admired at the Olympic. The nervous actor, heeding too well the equerry's instructions to 'Get out of the way as quick as you can', once presented, slipped away while the Queen was still speaking to him, whereupon she called 'Come back, Mr Robson, come back', waving her stick at him. The equerry had to retrieve him, and the Queen, laughing, eased the situation by referring to 'the great Robson'. Amongst the gifts later distributed to the actors, the finest, a pin set with sapphires, emeralds, and diamonds, went to the great Robson's relation.[30] The St James's Company ended their visit in the same high spirits with which it had begun, for after supping royally till the small hours, they sang 'For she's a jolly good fellow' as their charabanc passed what they assumed was the Queen's window on the way back to Ballater.[31]

The Queen's reaction to the playing she saw in her last twenty years was in keeping with her view of the players—both were a great deal more refined than she remembered. Her comment on the Kendals: 'They act beautifully, more in the French style than anything I have seen on the English stage',[32] clearly links them with her recollection of the 'Comédie Française à Londres', and the two little plays they performed also owed something to the *petites pièces* presented at the St James's in the 1840s and 1850s. On the other hand, when the Comédie Française itself played at Windsor in 1893, she recognized there was no substitute for the real thing: 'Between the pieces [*L'Eté de St Martin* and *La Joie Fait Peur*] M. Coquelin recited and gave some amusing monologues, so clever and witty, without the least vulgarity. There is nothing like the French for doing that kind of thing. We laughed very much.'[33] Her withdrawal from the theatre in 1861 had prevented her from seeing the Robertson comedies performed by the Bancrofts from 1865, but this loss was made up in some measure when she saw *Diplomacy* at Balmoral in 1893. Squire and Marie Bancroft had virtually retired from the stage for eight years, but John Hare had persuaded them to return for this revival of one of their biggest successes, and the Queen seems particularly to have enjoyed Marie's performance as Lady Henry Fairfax. 'Mrs Bancroft is a most clever and amusing actress, and her part, which in fact has nothing to do with the plot, helped to relieve the tension and severity of the piece.'[34] When the actress was presented after the performance, the Queen assured her: 'How you have made me laugh! and it is so nice to be merry.'[35] Perhaps she found confirmation of her view in the reactions of one of the guests, the exiled Empress Eugénie, then staying with the Prince and Princess of Wales at Abergeldie, another widow who had not seen a play for twenty-five years. [36]

The Journal does, however, draw some distinction between the refinement of the Kendals, Hare, and the Bancrofts, and the bolder methods of Henry Irving. The Queen admired him in *The Bells* and as Shylock, but her comment: 'The hero (Irving) though a mannerist of the Macready type, acted wonderfully',[37] seems to associate him with the past, rather than the new school. She also had some reservations about his Becket: 'Irving acted well, and with much dignity, but his elocution is not very distinct, especially when he gets excited'[38] (a fault others found in him throughout his career). In this production she criticized William Terriss as Henry II ('too noisy and violent') but admired Ellen Terry as Rosamund enormously: 'so graceful and so young-looking in her lovely light dress—quite wonderfully so, for she is 46!!'

As he did not appear until the second act in this play, Ellen Terry's son decided to explore:

I looked to right and left and came across a small ladder or stairway, going down under the stage. I am inquisitive about nothing on earth except matters to do with the Theatre; and I thought, 'Here is something I must look into; how is it held up, this stage?' I went down and looked around very quietly, for there was a slight buzz coming from the front of the house, where the ladies and gentlemen were assembled. So I advanced, bent double, looking right and left, till I came to a 'wall' made of a dark red curtain gathered into folds. 'I suppose that looks into the front of the theatre' thought I, and crept along, quietly as a cat, till I came to a division in the curtain. I parted the two sides very slightly, and peered through. And my eyes looked straight into those of Queen Victoria. There she sat, very comfortable, with nobody near her. I had a straight view of her—and you realise now that had I been anything but an old-fashioned Loyalist I could easily have shot the Good Queen dead! I would have been punished for it—how is it I was not rewarded at the time for *not* shooting her? I have been since.[39]

Although unaware of her mortal danger at this moment, the Queen was aware of Ellen Terry's past: 'A son of hers takes the part of a young Templar in the splendid Parliament scene.' If she found some fault with Irving's acting, she was full of praise for his presentation. At Sandringham 'The stage was beautifully arranged, with great scenic effects, and the pieces were splendidly mounted and with numbers of people taking part. I believe there were between 60 and 70, as well as the orchestra.' In *Becket* 'The staging is magnificent and Irving had all the scenery (there were many scenes) painted on purpose. The dresses and every detail were so correct and exact.'

The strong dramatic situation could still stir her: in *The Bells* 'The way in which Irving acted his own dream, and described the way in which he carried out the murder is wonderful and ghastly as well as the scene of his death. He had carried his secret about with him for 13 years!' and in Tennyson's play: 'The last scene, where Becket refuses to fly and defies his murderers, is very fine, and his death and the way he falls down the steps very striking.' Although *Diplomacy* confirmed the Queen's belief that 'it is so nice to be merry', it also reminded her that the theatre is a source of thrills: 'The scene in which "Julian" suspects his wife and she first discovers that he does so, her despair, and that it should be on their wedding day, were quite affecting.'[40] When Tree played *The Red Lamp* at Balmoral a year later, she noticed that it was 'very exciting and somewhat terrible, a little in the style of *Diplomacy* . . . Mr Tree is most wonderfully disguised as a fat old man of the Russian Secret Police, and acted admirably.'[41] He was then forty-one and still slim, so that the Queen's account of meeting him ends: 'Mr Tree I should never have recognised, he looks so different on the stage.'

The balance of the Command Performances, however, was heavily in favour of opera; the only two works the Queen asked to hear twice were *Carmen* and *Cavalleria Rusticana*, the Covent Garden Company appeared on eight occasions, the Carl Rosa twice (both at Balmoral and both in old royal favourites: *La Fille du Régiment* and *Fra Diavolo*). It may also be deduced that a third opera company, Richard D'Oyly Carte's, was largely responsible for the decision to make these Command Performances a regular feature of Court life. Their production of *The Gondoliers* (given towards the end of the original run at the Savoy) was the first presentation in the series at Windsor, and *The Mikado* was likewise the first of the Balmoral productions.

For the Queen to see *The Gondoliers* was doubtless a consummation of the hopes and happiness 'her' composer's career had given her. It was eight years since she had knighted Sullivan, and only two months since 'her' opera, *Ivanhoe*, had been successfully launched. She was proud of having sung some of Sullivan's music herself: E. F. Benson recalls her singing with Alick Yorke 'Prithee, pretty maiden' from *Patience*, 'in a very soft clear voice', and being 'much pleased with herself',[42] while of the *Gondoliers* performance she writes: 'The music, which I know and am very fond of, is quite charming.' Indeed the whole performance charmed her: the scenery ('The opening scene, with the Contadine singing and binding flowers, with a lovely view of Venice and the deep blue sea and sky, was really extraordinarily pretty'); such stalwart Savoyards as Jessie Bond ('a very clever little actress'), Rutland Barrington ('who is very fat'), and W. H. Denny; and the whole company ('in the last scene there were 80 people on the stage, which for an extemporised one, was wonderful').[43]

It was doubtless the success of *The Gondoliers* at Windsor that prompted the Queen six months later to command (apparently at forty-eight hours' notice)[44] a performance of *The Mikado* at Balmoral. Like so many sequels, the result seems to have been a little disappointing: 'The music is gay, but to my thinking, inferior to *The Gondoliers*, and though there are witty remarks and amusing topical allusions, the story is rather silly.'[45] Reasons for the anti-climax readily suggest themselves: the shortness of notice, different standards between the Savoy Theatre and the D'Oyly Carte 'C' Company; teething troubles in this first production at Balmoral. The Queen, however, makes no criticism of the performers. She praises George Thorne as Ko-Ko ('who jumped about most wonderfully'), Fred Billington as Pooh-Bah, and others; and notes that 'The Choruses were very good, the women good-looking.' Perhaps the secret of her disappointment lies in the phrase: 'the story is rather silly', which is often used in the Journal to mean 'it did not appeal to my sense of humour'. Gilbert's Mikado, one may assume, was not a monarch after Queen Victoria's heart.

In any case *The Gondoliers* and *The Mikado* had launched opera in this series of Command Performances, whereas it had played no part in the earlier Windsor series. Undoubtedly the Queen responded warmly, sometimes even passionately, to the operas old and new she now heard in performance. Among the new, perhaps the most surprisingly acceptable were the two she commanded twice: *Carmen* and *Cavalleria Rusticana*, both presenting ladies of easy virtue (Santuzza) or no virtue at all (Carmen). Yet the Queen now applied different standards of censorship to drama and opera. Tennyson's worthy but wordy tragedy had caused her some early misgivings:

The Queen is rather alarmed at hearing from the Princess of Wales and Prince George that there is some very strong language (disagreeable and coarse rather) in *Becket* which must be somewhat changed for performance *here* so close. Princess Louise says that some *scenes* or perhaps *one* are very *awkward*. What *can* be done?
   The Prince of Wales thought Sir Henry should see and speak to Irving.
   The Queen hates anything of that sort.[46]

but *Carmen* seems positively to have excited her curiosity. Her granddaughter, Marie (the Duke of Edinburgh's eldest girl), sat next to her. She was later to be Queen of Rumania and to publish several collections of romantic stories, as her literary style suggests:

I noticed that Grandmama was not only following the music with keen interest, but also the plot of the play. Somewhat bewildered by the passionate story, she kept asking me questions, which were not easy to answer owing to the loudness of the music and the unequal height of our chairs ... The first act over she turned to me for fuller explanations about the story. With a very young woman's diffidence I tried to impart to my grandparent my knowledge of Carmen's rather wild tale. Grandmama's smile broadened, this was the sort of story that did not often reach her ears.

Leaning towards me, her eyes full of dawning comprehension, she nevertheless pressed me for further explanations which, with flaming cheeks, I give as best I can. Grandmama raises her fan over her face, she is delightfully, pleasurably scandalised, but she understands; leaning towards me, her fan still over her mouth, she whispers: 'But, oh my dear child, I am afraid she's really not very nice!'[47]

The Queen did not relax her musical standards in these last years. The Escamillo in her first *Carmen* (1892) was Dufriche 'whose voice I do not admire'.[48] In *Trovatore* 'Tamagno, the celebrated Italian tenor, took the part of Manrico, and has a tremendously powerful voice, not at all suited to the part', while Giulia Ravogli 'sang well as Azucena, but the "timbre" of her voice is not pleasant'.[49] In the early *Cavelleria Rusticana* (1891) 'The Chorus was not of the best, but it did not spoil it.'[50] Nevertheless she praised far more often than she blamed, and in keeping with her early adulation of Grisi and Jenny Lind, it is the *prima donna* who usually earns both her admiration and affection.

Albani was a near neighbour at Balmoral, and in *Faust* (1894) she 'sang most beautifully and acts so touchingly, particularly in the Garden Scene'.[51] An American of French descent was her first Carmen:

Mlle Zélie de Lusan was a most perfect 'Carmen' and sang delightfully all the lovely pieces which fall to her part. She was beautifully dressed, and in the last scene wore a white mantilla and red rose in her hair. She acted admirably, full of byplay, and with a 'coquetterie' and impudence, accompanied by grace, so that it was never vulgar.[52]

Above all the Queen saw and was conquered by Emma Calvé, for whom she seems to have conceived an affection close to that she had felt for Jenny Lind. 'The great and admirable Calvé' played Santuzza in the second *Cavalleria Rusticana*, and

At the conclusion of the performance I went into the Green Drawingroom and everyone who had been invited passed by. Then Calvé came in with Mascagni, Sir A. Harris, and Tosti. She was still in her peasant's dress and looked tired. I praised her singing and acting very much, at which she seemed much pleased.[53]

A year later, in 1894, the Queen heard Calvé in the opera Massenet had written for her, *La Navarraise*. She found it 'very dramatic, but not pleasing, without much melody', although 'Calvé, for whom the opera was composed, was splendid as usual, in the wild character of Anita, and her mad laugh at the end, when her lover dies, is awful'. The Queen was clearly touched by the *diva's* solicitude for her feelings: 'Calvé came to the Drawingroom afterwards, looking so handsome. She feared I might have thought the opera too noisy and horrible.'[54]

The Journal suggests that these brief meetings with Calvé after the performance meant almost as much to the Queen as the performances themselves. Calvé played Carmen for her in 1895 'perfectly admirably and sang and acted most splendidly', but the highlight of the evening came later: 'Afterwards, as usual, I received the company in the Green Drawing Room, and when they had all passed Calvé came in, handsomer than ever and most amusing.'[55]

There was a four-year break in the Windsor performances after this *Carmen*, no doubt due largely to the sadness which descended on the Court following Prince Henry's death. In the spring of 1897 the Queen was staying on the Riviera at Cimiez, while Sarah Bernhardt and her company played an engagement in Nice. It was arranged that Bernhardt should give a performance of *Jean Marie* by Fleuriet in the Queen's suite at her hotel. It lasted only half an hour, but the Journal records: 'Sarah Bernhardt's acting was quite marvellous, so pathetic and full of feeling. She appeared much affected herself, tears rolling down her cheeks.' At the end, 'When I expressed the hope that she was not tired, she answered: "Cela m'a reposée".'[56] Doubtless the Queen echoed her sentiment.

Before Prince Henry's death a tradition had been established of a Windsor performance on or near the Queen's birthday: in 1894 *Faust*, in 1895 *Il Trovatore* ('I'm very grateful for having spent such a happy birthday, and having had so much kindness shown me').[57] On 24 May 1899 the Queen was eighty, and the occasion warranted a revival of the tradition. The Covent Garden Company were commanded to perform extracts from *Lohengrin*, with Jean de Reszke as Lohengrin and Edouard de Reszke as Heinrich der Vogler, and it proved an inspired choice. At last the Queen could see a Wagner opera in performance:

I was simply enchanted. It is the most glorious composition, so poetic, so dramatic, as one might almost say, religious in feeling, and full of sadness, pathos and tenderness. Jean de Reszke so handsome in his white attire, armour and helmet, and the electric light was turned strong upon him, so that he seemed surrounded by a halo. The whole opera produced a great impression on me . . . It was a fine ending to this memorable day.[58]

Lohengrin was not quite the Queen's last attendance at a theatrical performance. Six weeks later she saw a double bill, one item very old (Adam's *Le Chalet*—'un peu naif' records the Journal—the other nearly new, *Pagliacci* ('I still prefer the *Cavalleria*, though this is perhaps the more powerful composition').[59] But for a royal swan-song *Lohengrin* was perfect, literally and figuratively. As a young girl, the Queen had found balm for her wounds and hope for the future in the Magic Box of the theatre. As an old woman, less than two years from her death, she carried with her to the grave the vision of Jean de Reszke as Lohengrin, 'so handsome in his white attire, armour and helmet, and the electric light was turned strong upon him, so that he seemed surrounded by a halo'.

8

Accolade

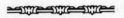

In the latter half of Queen Victoria's reign honours for the arts were increasingly conferred and applauded. There was a peerage for Tennyson, a knighthood for Sullivan, another for Leighton (converted into a peerage on his deathbed) and for Alma-Tadema, a baronetcy for Millais, despite his having eloped with Ruskin's wife. As has been seen, the Crown's encouragement of the theatre from the time of the Windsor Theatricals led to press speculation on a knighthood for Charles Kean in the mid 1850s, but these hopes came to nothing, and for another thirty years the acting profession remained unrecognized. By the 1880s predictions were again being made. On 27 June 1883, eighteen months after the Marlborough House dinner, Gladstone addressed a private enquiry to the Lord Chief Justice: 'Would it be too audacious to offer Irving a knighthood? Please let this be most secret: for I should have to hold divers consultations before acting.'[1] Stephen Coleridge, the Lord Chief Justice's son and an intimate of Irving's, brought back a polite refusal. In the actor's view the theatre was still a 'commonwealth' in which there was no place for an overlord:

He would not accept it; he said that an actor differed from other artists, musicians and the like, in that he had to appear in person every night appealing directly to the public favour ... that there was a fellowship among actors of a company that would be impaired by any elevation of one member over another; that his strength as a manager and power as an actor lay far more in the suffrages of the plain folk in the pit than in the patronage, however lofty, of the great people; that he knew instinctively that large numbers of these same plain folk would be offended at their simple Henry Irving accepting decorations of a titular kind.[2]

That twelve years later and under another Prime Minister, Lord Rosebery, Irving should have changed his mind could be largely due to the increasing frequency of Command Performances at Court: not only by the Lyceum Company but also by his colleagues and competitors (Bancroft, Kendal, Hare, Tree, Alexander) and even more frequently by operatic *confrères*. It is, however, significant that the only two actors to be knighted by Queen Victoria were Irving and Bancroft, both prominent in the decades which preceded the reintroduction of Command Performances. Even Charles Wyndham, an actor of their generation, was apparently excluded in 1897, after a tentative approach had been made to him,[3] perhaps because at that time he was still remembered as the purveyor of *risqué* farces like *Brighton* and *Pink Dominos*. Not until the freer atmosphere of Edward VII's reign was Wyndham to be knighted, along with Hare and Tree, and amongst dramatists Gilbert and Pinero.

The retrospective character of the honours recommended to the Queen reflects the conservative character of the plays chosen by and for her. She saw (amongst lesser pieces) *The Bells, Diplomacy*, and *A Pair of Spectacles*, all second-hand goods taken from the French, and all public favourites of that slack-water period of English drama between one high tide (Robertson's comedies) and another (the society dramas of Wilde, Pinero, and Jones). She saw most of *Becket*, but only one scene from *The Merchant of Venice*. She did *not* see *Lady Windermere's Fan, The Second Mrs Tanqueray*, or *The Case of Rebellious Susan*, still less *Mrs Warren's Profession* or *Ghosts* (which her Lord Chamberlain would not have allowed), or even *Arms and the Man* and *Candida*, which he would.

It would, however, be idle to condemn or even consider too seriously the limitation of choice for the Command Performances of the 1890s. The Queen was not only a widow, but a great-grandmother approaching her eighties, and anyone with these attributes has anxieties and sorrows enough without the theatre forcing others upon her. Even today the choice of a film for the Royal Command Performance leaves everyone dissatisfied (including, perhaps, the members of the Royal Family graciously attending it), except those financially responsible for the film itself, and the selected charity.

Although delayed and limited, the knighthoods conferred on Irving and Bancroft nevertheless placed a royal—and real—recognition on the progress of the theatre during Queen Victoria's reign. Irving correctly judged the change in public and professional feeling between

1883 and 1895. By the latter date he was not only still unchallengeably *primus* of his profession, but now *primus inter pares*; the ranks of the actor-managers had been swelled by younger, no less worthy men, the numbers of theatres had been increased—to such long-frequented houses as the Haymarket, the St James's, and the Lyceum, had been added in the preceding twenty years the newer Comedy, Savoy, and Court amongst others, and the audiences were growing steadily more numerous, more respectable, more discriminating. The theatre remained, as it had always been, a craft; but it had become (as it had not always been recognized) an art, practised by men of taste and responsibility. Presumably the announcement of Irving's knighthood was planned weeks before 25 May 1895; that it preceded by two days the sentencing of Oscar Wilde, the most sensationally successful playwright of the past four seasons, to two years penal servitude with hard labour, was wholly fortuitous. It is, nevertheless, a tribute to Irving and his profession that far from being postponed, the announcement of his knighthood was greeted next day by a roar of congratulations from all over the world.[4]

In a famous essay mourning Irving's death Max Beerbohm remembered seeing him pass by in a brougham on the way to Paddington Station, to entrain for Windsor, the castle, his Queen, and the accolade:

That day, when I saw him on his way to Windsor, and tried to imagine just what impression he would make on Queen Victoria, I found myself thinking of the impression made there by Disraeli; and I fancied that the two impressions might be rather similar. Both men were courtiers, yet incongruous in a court. And both had a certain dandyism—the arrangement of their hair and the fashion of their clothes carefully thought out in reference to their appearance and their temperament. And both, it seemed to me, had something of dandyism in the wider, philosophic sense of the word—were men whose whole life was ordered with a certain ceremonial, as courtly functions are ordered . . . And, above all, both men preserved in the glare of fame that quality of mystery which is not essential to genius, but which is the safest insurance against oblivion. It has been truly said that Irving would have been eminent in any walk of life. Had Disraeli the Younger drifted from literature to the foot-lights, and had Henry Brodribb strayed from the schoolroom into politics, I daresay that neither our political nor our theatrical history would be very different from what it is—except in the matter of dates.[5]

If, indeed, Irving did remind the Queen of her favourite Prime Minister, that may account for her breaking with precedent (according to an Irving family tradition) and pronouncing the words: 'I am very, very pleased', as she touched the actor's shoulders with the sword.[6]

She did not break with precedent so far as to breach the confidence of that moment in her Journal, which merely reads: 'After luncheon I knighted the following 19 people', and lists 'Mr Henry Irving' along with 'Mr Walter Besant' and 'Mr Jehangier Cowasgee Jehangier'.[7] Nor was she less discreet, two years later, when Squire Bancroft journeyed across the water to Osborne to be similarly honoured in a manifestly Diamond Jubilee list, on which 'Squire B. Bancroft Esq.' is in the company of the Lord Mayor of York, the mayors of Brighton, Norwich, and Salford, the sheriffs of Birmingham and the City of London, and 'the late President of the Calcutta Chamber of Commerce'.[8]

Ten weeks before the announcement of Irving's knighthood, the Queen sent word by Sir Henry Ponsonby that she wished to receive in audience an actress who had made her début in 1825. As Mary Ann Goward she had delighted the Queen from her earliest visits to the theatre. As Mrs Keeley she had played Nerissa to Ellen Kean's Portia on the first night of the Windsor Theatricals. With her husband, Robert Keeley, she had given the Queen more pleasure over many more years than any other living performer. She was then in her ninetieth year. When the royal summons arrived, the recipient had two instant reactions: 'I can't afford a new dress; my black will have to do.' 'I can't curtsey; I am at present suffering tortures from my rheumatic leg, and stooping would be impossible. I will bow as much as you like, but I can do no more.'[9]

The Queen, apprised of the difficulty, insisted that she 'enter as best she could'. The audience was graced by the presence of the Dowager Empress of Germany (a widow for six years now) and Princess Louise, both of whom as children had laughed and clapped their hands at the antics of the Keeleys. As she drew herself up to leave, the old actress asked: 'May I kiss your hand, ma'am?' She was warmly encouraged to do so.[10] Twenty years later the Queen's grandson honoured as a Dame of the British Empire the actress who, when a girl of ten, had delighted her sovereign as Puck in Charles Kean's production of *A Midsummer Night's Dream*: Ellen Terry.

The knighthoods conferred on Irving and Bancroft sum up Queen Victoria's official theatregoing: State visits, Windsor Theatricals, Command Performances—all added up to a reversal of attitude from condemnation of players as rogues and vagabonds to recognition as artists and servants of the public. Her personal theatregoing can perhaps be more simply expressed. From the age of twelve to the age of forty-two she found in the theatre joy, magic, release, worship. For the next twenty years of her life she sacrificed all these on the altar of widowhood. In the last twenty years she came, cautiously but thankfully, to accept again some measure of the delight the theatre could bring her. Since the popular image of the Queen in middle and old age is of a black-gowned, stern-faced monarch and matriarch, it may be timely to see her, whether a girl, young wife and mother, or indulgent grandmother, as a spectator, laughing at and loving the performance of a favourite opera or play. She was not only amused; she was grateful and appreciative. She was a theatregoer.

Notes

Chapter 1   THE MAGIC BOX

1   Viscount Esher, editor: *The Girlhood of Queen Victoria*, 1912 (henceforward *Girlhood*) vol. I, 154.
2   *Girlhood*, I, 56.
3   Royal Archives, Windsor Castle, Queen Victoria's Journal (henceforward RA (Q.V. Journal)), 8 February 1850.
4   *Girlhood*, I, 57.
5   ibid., 97.
6   ibid.
7   ibid., 75.
8   ibid., 79–80.
9   ibid., 93.
10 ibid., 94.
11 ibid., 111.
12 ibid., 121.
13 ibid., 114.
14 ibid., 115–16.
15 ibid., 133.
16 RA (Q.V. Journal), 10 August 1836.
17 Quoted by Cecil Woodham-Smith: *Queen Victoria. Her Life and Times*, 1972, vol. I, 129.
18 *Girlhood*, I, 88.
19 ibid., 147.
20 ibid., 148.
21 ibid., 149.
22 ibid., 149–50.

Chapter 2   'LORD M. SAID ...'

1   *Girlhood*, II, 128.
2   ibid., II, 90.
3   ibid., I, 235.
4   ibid., II, 84.
5   ibid.

6 ibid.
7 ibid., II, 10–11.
8 ibid., II, 183.
9 ibid., I, 256.
10 RA (Q.V. Journal), 15 November 1837.
11 *Girlhood*, I, 236–7.
12 RA (Q.V. Journal), 5 December 1837.
13 *Girlhood*, I, 266.
14 ibid., I, 272.
15 ibid., I, 266.
16 ibid., I, 267.
17 ibid., I, 256.
18 ibid., II, 122.
19 ibid., I, 269–70.
20 RA (Q.V. Journal), 18 December 1837.
21 *Girlhood*, I, 265–6.
22 ibid., I, 271.
23 ibid., I, 272.
24 ibid., II, 32.
25 ibid., I, 330.
26 ibid., II, 92.
27 ibid., II, 127.
28 ibid., II, 127.
29 ibid., I, 292.
30 *The Diaries of William Charles Macready*, edited by William Toynbee, 1912 (henceforward *Diaries*), I, 446–7.
31 Charles H. Shattuck, editor: *Bulwer and Macready. A Chronicle of the Early Victorian Theatre*, 1958, 75.
32 RA (Q.V. Journal), 6 March 1838.
33 ibid., 1 February 1839.
34 *Diaries*, I, 495.
35 RA (Q.V. Journal), 5 February 1839.
36 ibid., 9 March 1839.
37 ibid., 15 July 1839.
38 *Girlhood*, II, 217–18.
39 RA (Q.V. Journal), 10 January 1839.
40 *Girlhood*, II, 105–6.
41 RA (Q.V. Journal), 24 January 1839.
42 ibid., 29 January 1838.
43 *Diaries*, I, 492–3.
44 RA (Q.V. Journal), 1 February 1839.
45 *Diaries*, I, 496.
46 RA (Q.V. Journal), 25 June 1839.

Chapter 3 FIRST PERSON PLURAL

1 *Victoria R.I.*, 1964, 129.
2 Theodore Martin: *The Life of the Prince Consort*, 1875, vol. I, 86.

3   RA (Q.V. Journal), 26 February 1840.
4   ibid., 28 February 1840.
5   ibid., 13 June 1840.
6   ibid., 27 June 1850.
7   ibid., 17 June 1848.
8   ibid., 3 May 1838.
9   ibid., 16 April 1839.
10 ibid., 17 May 1839.
11 ibid., 5 April 1838.
12 ibid., 26 April 1845.
13 ibid., 29 July 1843.
14 ibid., 24 April 1847.
15 ibid., 23 March 1849.
16 ibid., 16 June 1838.
17 ibid., 20 March 1841.
18 ibid., 13 July 1839.
19 ibid., 6 August 1839.
20 ibid., 17 April 1847.
21 ibid., 19 March 1850.
22 ibid., 13 April 1847.
23 ibid., 22 July 1847.
24 ibid., 17 June 1854.
25 ibid., 31 May 1856.
26 ibid., 8 May 1860.
27 ibid., 12 May 1855.
28 ibid., 6 May 1847.
29 ibid., 3 July 1847.
30 ibid., 10 July 1847.
31 ibid., 12 June 1847.
32 ibid., 15 June 1847.
33 ibid., 19 June 1852.
34 ibid., 25 June 1853.
35 ibid., 10 July 1851.
36 ibid., 31 March 1841.
37 ibid., 17 July 1845.
38 ibid., 10 August 1839.
39 ibid., 20 May 1845.
40 ibid., 19 March 1847.
41 ibid., 26 January 1846.
42 ibid., 17 July 1845
43 ibid., 29 March 1838.
44 ibid., 17 July 1845.
45 ibid., 3 July 1841.
46 ibid., 3 March 1840.
47 ibid., 10 April 1840.
48 ibid., 5 February 1841.
49 ibid., 9 March 1842.
50 ibid., 29 April 1842.

51 ibid., 26 February 1841.
52 ibid., 6 March 1841.
53 ibid., 11 March 1842.
54 ibid., 4 April 1842.
55 ibid., 18 March 1842.
56 *Diaries*, II, 212.
57 ibid.
58 Roger Fulford, editor: *Dearest Child: Letters between Queen Victoria and the Princess Royal*, 1964, 183.
59 RA (Q.V. Journal), 27 February 1843.
60 ibid., 4 June 1841.
61 ibid., 2 June 1841.
62 ibid., 6 June 1851.
63 ibid., 22 July 1851.
64 ibid., 23 July 1847.
65 ibid., 4 May 1842.
66 ibid., 4 June 1847.
67 ibid., 9 June 1851.
68 ibid., 3 March 1845.
69 ibid., 24 February 1845.
70 ibid., 22 March 1852.
71 ibid., 19 January 1847.
72 ibid., 23 July 1847.
73 Douglas R. Vander Yacht: 'Politics and Royal Patronage' in *Ohio State University Theatre Bulletin*, 1970, 32–9.
74 Folger Shakespeare Library: 'Kean Correspondence' Y.c. 393 (131), quoted by Vander Yacht loc. cit., 39.

Chapter 4 WELCOME TO WINDSOR

1   H. Bolitho, editor: *Further Letters of Queen Victoria*, 1938, 15.
2   *Theatrical Chronicle*, 30 December 1848.
3   ibid.
4   RA (Q.V. Journal), 28 December 1848.
5   ibid., 11 January 1849.
6   George Ellis: 'Expenses, Royal Dramatic Performances, Windsor Castle, Charles Kean, Director' in Folger Shakespeare Library.
7   RA (Q.V. Journal), 2 February 1854.
8   ibid., 4 February 1853.
9   ibid., 10 January 1856.
10 ibid., 28 December 1848.
11 *Random Recollections of an Old Actor*, 1880, 159–60.
12 RA (Q.V. Journal), 10 November 1853.
13 op. cit., 159.
14 RA (Q.V. Journal), 21 November 1855.
15 ibid., 15 January 1857.
16 RA Add Y/48, 9 January 1853.
17 William W. Appleton: *Madame Vestris and the London Stage*, 1974, 177.

18 RA (Q.V. Journal), 1 February 1850.
19 Reprinted in J. W. Cole: *The Life and Theatrical Times of Charles Kean, FSA*, 1859, vol. II, 195–6.
20 RA (Q.V. Journal), 6 February 1852.
21 ibid., 28 December 1848.
22 ibid., 1 February 1850.
23 ibid., 7 January 1853.
24 ibid., 10 November 1853.
25 ibid., 31 January 1851.
26 ibid., 28 April 1856.
27 ibid., 18 February 1853.
28 ibid., 5 June 1855.
29 ibid.
30 *The Leader*, 19 February 1853; reprinted in George Rowell, editor: *Victorian Dramatic Criticism*, 1971, 95.
31 ibid., 4 February 1853.
32 ibid., 24 January 1852.
33 ibid., 26 March 1852.
34 ibid., 2 May 1854.
35 ibid., 2 June 1852.
36 ibid., 19 April 1852.
37 ibid., 28 December 1848.
38 ibid., 11 January 1849.
39 ibid., 31 January 1851.
40 ibid., 7 January 1853.
41 ibid., 12 January 1854.
42 ibid., 19 January 1854.
43 J. W. Cole: op. cit., 245.
44 ibid., 293.
45 Roger Fulford, editor: *Dearest Child*, 172.
46 RA (Q.V. Journal), 19 January 1858.
47 George Ellis: loc. cit.
48 RA A246, 3 December 1859.
49 RA A246, 20 November 1859.
50 RA A246, 7 December 1859.
51 RA A246, 13 December 1859.
52 Library of University of Rochester, USA. Letter dated 29 December 1848.
53 Walter Goodman: *The Keeleys on the Stage and at Home*, 1895, 213.
54 RA (Q.V. Journal), 14 January 1853.
55 ibid., 16 January 1852.
56 ibid., 30 November 1859.
57 ibid., 24 January 1861.
58 ibid., 11 January 1860.
59 Letter to W. B. Donne, dated 25 March 1860, in the Philbrick Library, Los Altos Hills, USA.
60 RA 7061, 25 February 1861.
61 RA 7061, 26 April 1861.

Chapter 5 FAMILY FAVOURITES

1 Roger Fulford, editor: *Dearest Child*, 183.
2 RA (Q.V. Journal), 2 June 1852.
3 ibid., 5 June 1852.
4 ibid., 22 June 1852.
5 ibid., 2 July 1852.
6 ibid., 11 May 1847.
7 ibid., 21 April 1846.
8 H. Saxe-Wyndham: *Annals of Covent Garden Theatre*, 1905, vol. II, 213–14.
9 RA (Q.V. Journal), 6 February 1852.
10 ibid., 17 February 1857.
11 ibid., 10 March 1852.
12 ibid., 23 March 1844.
13 *Dearest Child*, 183.
14 ibid., 178.
15 ibid., 152.
16 RA (Q.V. Journal), 16 May 1851.
17 ibid., 4 July 1857.
18 ibid., 3 February 1851.
19 ibid., 22 February 1855.
20 ibid., 17 February 1854.
21 ibid., 12 August 1854.
22 ibid., 24 February 1853.
23 ibid., 21 February 1850.
24 ibid., 16 February 1852.
25 ibid., 13 February 1851.
26 ibid., 16 February 1852.
27 ibid., 27 April 1852.
28 ibid., 21 March 1854.
29 ibid., 6 April 1854.
30 *Dearest Child*, 191.
31 RA (Q.V. Journal), 26 June 1855.
32 ibid., 28 January 1856.
33 ibid., 20 February 1855.
34 ibid., 18 February 1856.
35 ibid., 28 February 1859.
36 *Dearest Child*, 233.

Chapter 6 THEATRE ROYAL

1 Arthur Ponsonby: *Henry Ponsonby: His Life from his Letters*, 1942, 122.
2 RA (Q.V. Journal), 10 February 1852.
3 ibid.
4 ibid.
5 ibid., 11 January 1853.
6 ibid.
7 ibid.

8 ibid., 6 January 1852.
9 ibid., 10 February 1853.
10 ibid., 30 January 1855.
11 ibid., 16 January 1854.
12 RA PPZ/5/4323.
13 RA (Q.V. Journal), 10 February 1854.
14 ibid., 9 February 1856.
15 ibid., 10 February 1860.
16 Victor Mallet, editor: *Life with Queen Victoria: Marie Mallet's letters from Court 1887–1901*, 1968, xvi.
17 RA (Q.V. Journal), 22 June 1889.
18 ibid., 23 June 1889.
19 James Pope-Hennessy: *Queen Mary*, 1959, 206.
20 Frederick Ponsonby: *Recollections of Three Reigns*, 1951, 51.
21 see Arthur Ponsonby: op. cit., 84.
22 RA (Q.V. Journal), 24 October 1893.
23 ibid., 25 October 1893.
24 James Pope-Hennessy: *Queen Victoria at Windsor and Balmoral*, 1954, 72.
25 Victor Mallet: op. cit., 15.
26 ibid.
27 RA (Q.V. Journal), 6 January 1888.
28 ibid., 5 October 1888.
29 H. J. Greenwall: *The Strange Life of Willie Clarkson*, 1936, 65.
30 RA (Q.V. Journal), 20 January 1890.
31 ibid., 8 October 1890.
32 ibid., 6 October 1888.
33 ibid., 8 June 1893.
34 ibid., 24 May 1893.
35 ibid., 8 January 1891.
36 ibid., 5 October 1888.
37 ibid., 2 May 1894.
38 ibid., 5 October 1889.
39 ibid., 7 October 1890.
40 Alan Hardy: *Queen Victoria was Amused*, 1976, 172.

Chapter 7 THE QUEEN COMMANDS

1 Arthur Ponsonby: op. cit., 83.
2 Laurence Irving: *Henry Irving: The Actor and his World*, 1951, 220.
3 ibid., 254.
4 ibid., 468.
5 ibid., 407.
6 Philip Magnus: *King Edward the Seventh*, 1964, 219.
7 ibid., 109.
8 ibid., 172.
9 ibid., 173.
10 See Jane W. Stedman: 'The Genesis of *Patience*', reprinted in W. S. Gilbert: *A Century of Scholarship and Commentary*, edited by John Bush Jones, 1970.

11 *The Era*, vol. 44 no. 2246, 8 October 1881, 8.
12 ibid.
13 ibid.
14 RA (Q.V. Journal), 4 October 1881.
15 *The Era:* loc. cit.
16 Laurence Irving: op. cit., 512.
17 *Index to the Story of My Days*, 1957, 144.
18 See Iain Watson: 'Royal Command' in the *Gilbert and Sullivan Journal*, vol. X, no. 11, 1976, 230–2.
19 Hesketh Pearson: *Beerbohm Tree: His Life and Laughter*, 1956, 79.
20 Madge Kendal: *Dame Madge Kendal, by Herself*, 1933, 205–12.
21 RA (Q.V. Journal), 26 April 1889.
22 ibid., 26 October 1893.
23 ibid., 15 January 1857.
24 Kendal: op. cit., 205.
25 RA (Q.V. Journal), 26 April 1889.
26 ibid., 17 March 1891.
27 ibid., 16 September 1895.
28 *Candied Peel: Tales without Prejudice*, 1931, 144–8.
29 ibid., 146.
30 ibid., 148.
31 ibid.
32 RA (Q.V. Journal), 1 February 1887.
33 G. E. Buckle, editor: *Letters of Queen Victoria*, series III, vol. 2, 1930, 267.
34 RA (Q.V. Journal), 26 October 1893.
35 Squire Bancroft: *The Bancrofts: Recollections of Sixty Years*, 1909, 342.
36 ibid., 341.
37 RA (Q.V. Journal), 26 April 1889.
38 ibid., 18 March 1893.
39 op. cit., 145.
40 RA (Q.V. Journal), 26 October 1893.
41 ibid., 25 September 1894.
42 E. F. Benson: *As We Were*, 1930, 33.
43 RA (Q.V. Journal), 6 March 1891.
44 Iain Watson: loc. cit.
45 RA (Q.V. Journal), 4 September 1891.
46 Arthur Ponsonby: op. cit., 82–3.
47 *The Story of My Life*, 1934, vol. I, 255.
48 RA (Q.V. Journal), 3 December 1892.
49 ibid., 24 March 1895.
50 ibid., 26 November 1891.
51 ibid., 19 May 1894.
52 ibid., 3 December 1892.
53 ibid., 15 July 1893.
54 ibid., 6 July 1894.
55 ibid., 16 July 1895.
56 *Letters of Queen Victoria*, series III, vol. 3, 151.
57 RA (Q.V. Journal), 24 May 1895.

58   ibid., 24 May 1899.
59   ibid., 4 July 1899.

Chapter 8   ACCOLADE

 1   Lawrence Irving: op. cit., 410.
 2   ibid.
 3   Mary Moore: *Charles Wyndham and Mary Moore*, 1925, 154–5.
 4   Irving: op. cit., 578.
 5   Reprinted in *Around Threatres*, 1953, 400–1.
 6   Irving: op. cit., 578.
 7   RA (Q.V. Journal), 18 July 1895.
 8   ibid., 18 August 1897.
 9   Walter Goodman: op. cit., 329.
10   ibid.

Bibliography

(The place of publication is London unless otherwise stated)

William W. Appleton: *Madame Vestris and the London Stage* (New York, 1974)
Sir Squire Bancroft: *The Bancrofts: Recollections of Sixty Years* (1909)
Sir Max Beerbohm: *Around Theatres* (1953)
Fred Belton: *Random Recollections of an Old Actor* (1880)
E. F. Benson: *As We Were* (1930)
Ian Bevan: *Royal Performance: The Story of Royal Theatregoing* (1954)
Hector Bolitho (editor): *Further Letters of Queen Victoria* (1938)
Michael R. Booth: 'Queen Victoria and the Theatre', *University of Toronto Quarterly* XXXVI (Toronto, April 1967).
J. K. Chapman: *A Complete History of Royal Dramatic Entertainments* (?1848)
J. W. Cole: *The Life and Theatrical Times of Charles Kean FSA* (1859, 2 vols.)
Gordon Craig: *Index to the Story of My Days* (1957)
Alan S. Downer: *The Eminent Tragedian: William Charles Macready* (Cambridge, Mass., 1966)
Viscount Esher (editor): *The Girlhood of Queen Victoria: A Selection from Her Majesty's Diaries between the Years 1832 and 1840* (1912, 2 vols.)
Roger Fulford (editor): *Dearest Child: Letters between Queen Victoria and the Princess Royal 1858–1861* (1964)
Walter Goodman: *The Keeleys On the Stage and At Home* (1895)
H. J. Greenwall: *The Strange Life of Willie Clarkson* (1936)
Alan Hardy: *Queen Victoria Was Amused* (1976)
Lawrence Irving: *Henry Irving: The Actor and His World* (1951)
Michael Jamieson: 'An American Actress at Balmoral', *Theatre Research International* vol. II, no. 2 (1977)
Dame Madge Kendal: *Dame Madge Kendal, By Herself* (1933)
Elizabeth Longford: *Victoria R.I.* (1964)
William Charles Macready: *The Diaries of William Charles Macready 1833–1851* edited by William Toynbee (1912, 2 vols.)
Philip Magnus: *King Edward the Seventh* (1964)
Victor Mallet (editor): *Life with Queen Victoria: Marie Mallet's Letters from Court 1887–1901* (1968)
Marie, Queen of Rumania: *The Story of My Life* (1934, 2 vols.)
Sir Theodore Martin: *The Life of the Prince Consort* (1875–1880, 5 vols.)

Bibliography

Mary Moore: *Charles Wyndham and Mary Moore* (1925)

Allardyce Nicoll: *A History of English Drama 1660–1900:* vol. IV *Early Nineteenth Century Drama 1800–1850* (Cambridge, 1955); vol. V *Late Nineteenth Century Drama 1850–1900* (Cambridge, 1959)

Hesketh Pearson: *Beerbohm Tree: His Life and Laughter* (1956)

F. Kinsey Peile: *Candied Peel: Tales without Prejudice* (1931)

Arthur Ponsonby: *Henry Ponsonby: His Life from His Letters* (1942)

Frederick Ponsonby: *Recollections of Three Reigns* (1951)

James Pope-Hennessy: *Queen Mary* (1959)

James Pope-Hennessy: *Queen Victoria at Windsor and Balmoral* (1954)

George Rowell (editor): *Victorian Dramatic Criticism* (1971)

George Rowell: *The Victorian Theatre: A Survey* (1967)

H. Saxe-Wyndham: *Annals of Covent Garden Theatre* (1905, 2 vols.)

Charles H. Shattuck (editor): *Bulwer and Macready: A Chronicle of the Early Victorian Theatre* (Urbana, Illinois, 1958)

Jane W. Stedman: 'The Genesis of *Patience*', reprinted in *W. S. Gilbert: A Century of Scholarship and Commentary*, edited by John Bush Jones (New York, 1970)

Douglas R. Vander Yacht: 'Politics and Royal Patronage', *Ohio State University Theatre Bulletin* (Columbus, Ohio, 1970)

Victoria, H.M. Queen: *Letters of Queen Victoria*, 1st series, edited by A. C. Benson and Viscount Esher (1908, 3 vols.); 2nd series, edited by G. E. Buckle (1926–1928, 3 vols.); 3rd series, edited by G. E. Buckle (1930–1932, 3 vols.)

Iain Watson: 'Royal Command', *Gilbert and Sullivan Journal*, vol. X, no. 11 (1976)

Cecil Woodham-Smith: *Queen Victoria: Her Life and Times*, vol. I (1972)

APPENDIX

A Calendar of
Queen Victoria's Theatregoing

The following lists make no claim to be comprehensive. They are derived chiefly from sources in the Royal Archives, Windsor Castle, and attempt to indicate the pattern and frequency of the Queen's visits to the theatre.

Only items in the programme of which some evidence exists that the Queen witnessed a portion have been included, but no indication is given as to whether she saw the whole item, or whether the item itself was an extract.

Theatres are abbreviated as follows:

HM   Her Majesty's
CG   Covent Garden
DL   Drury Lane
Hay   Theatre Royal, Haymarket
Lyc   Lyceum
St J.   St James's
Olymp   Olympic
Pcess   Princess's

1837

15 Nov DL *Siege of la Rochelle; Simpson & Co.*
17 Nov CG *Werner; Fra Diavolo*
23 Nov Lyc *L'Elisir d'Amore; L'Inganno Felice; Campanello*
5 Dec DL *Joan of Arc; Daughter of the Danube*
7 Dec CG *Amilie; Joan of Arc*
9 Dec Lyc *Italiana in Algieri; Nicora Figaro*
18 Dec CG *Macbeth; Joan of Arc*
23 Dec Lyc *Scaramuccia*

1838

23 Jan Lyc *Betty; Scaramuccia*
26 Jan DL *Hamlet; Jack-a-Lantern*
3 Feb Lyc *Elisa & Claudio*

5 Feb DL *Richard III; Jack-a-Lantern*
8 Feb Lyc *L'Elisir; Betty*
1 Mar DL *Richard III; Sonnambula*
3 Mar CG *Lady of Lyons; Irish Ambassador; Omnibus*
6 Mar CG *Lady of Lyons*
29 Mar HM *Sonnambula*
5 Apr HM *Lucia di Lammermoor*
7 Apr HM *Lucia di Lammermoor*
24 Apr HM *Otello*
26 Apr HM *Puritani; Sonnambula*
28 Apr HM *Puritani*
3 May HM *Norma*
5 May HM *Norma*
8 May HM *Puritani*
12 May HM *Lucia di Lammermoor*

128

22 May HM *Sonnambula; Norma*
26 May HM *Norma; Lucia di Lammermoor*
5 June HM *Parisina*
9 June HM *Parisina*
16 June HM *Matilda di Shabran; Le Naufrage*
26 June HM *Parisina; Cachucha; Sonnambula*
3 July HM *Puritani; Le Naufrage*
7 July HM *Figaro*
10 July HM *Malek Adel*
14 July HM *Malek Adel*
21 July HM *Falstaff*
24 July HM *Puritani; Cachucha*
28 July HM *Norma*
31 July HM *Lucia di Lammermoor*
4 Aug HM *Falstaff*
7 Aug HM *Gazza Ladra*
11 Aug HM *Puritani*
18 Aug HM *Figaro; Anna Bolena*

1839
10 Jan DL *Harlequin & Jack Frost;* Van Amburgh's Lions
15 Jan Hay *Irish Ambassador; O'Flanagan & the Fairies; Tom Noddy's Secret*
17 Jan DL *Harlequin & Jack Frost;* Van Amburgh's Lions
18 Jan CG *Rob Roy McGregor; Harlequin & Fair Rosamund*
24 Jan DL *Harlequin & Jack Frost;* Van Amburgh's Lions
29 Jan DL *Maid of Artois;* Van Amburgh's Lions
1 Feb CG *Lady of Lyons; Rob Roy McGregor*
4 Feb DL *William Tell;* Van Amburgh's Lions
5 Feb CG *Tempest; Harlequin & Fair Rosamund*
12 Feb DL *Farinelli;* Van Amburgh's Lions
14 Feb CG *Lady of Lyons; King & Duke*
18 Feb CG *King Lear*
23 Feb CG *William Tell*
26 Feb DL *Farinelli;* Van Amburgh's Lions
9 Mar CG *Richelieu*
14 Mar CG *Richelieu; Fra Diavolo*
2 Apr Hay *Born to Good Luck; Irish Lion*
3 Apr DL *Little Hunchback; King of the Mist*
8 Apr DL *Gazza Ladra; Devil on 2 Sticks*
9 Apr HM *Puritani*
13 Apr HM *La Sonnambula*
16 Apr HM *Gazza Ladra*
20 Apr HM *Lucia di Lammermoor; Une Nuit de Bal*
23 Apr HM *Puritani*

27 Apr HM *Anna Bolena; Une Nuit de Bal*
30 Apr HM *Anna Bolena*
11 May HM *Anna Bolena*
17 May HM *Otello*
21 May HM *Figaro*
25 May HM *Otello*
1 June HM *Anna Bolena*
8 June HM *Lucrezia Borgia; La Gitana*
11 June HM *Lucrezia Borgia*
15 June HM *Cenerentola*
18 June HM *Lucrezia Borgia; La Gitana*
22 June HM *Otello; La Gitana*
25 June HM *Otello; La Gitana*
29 June HM *Lucrezia Borgia; La Gitana*
2 July HM *Lucrezia Borgia; La Gitana*
13 July HM *Guillaume Tell*
15 July CG *Henry V*
16 July HM *Guillaume Tell; La Gitana*
20 July HM *Puritani*
23 July HM *Lucrezia Borgia; Lucia di Lammermoor*
27 July HM *Norma; The Gipsy*
30 July HM *Norma*
1 Aug HM *Lucia di Lammermoor; The Gipsy*
3 Aug HM *Puritani*
6 Aug HM *Guillaume Tell*
10 Aug HM *Don Giovanni*
15 Aug Hay *King O'Neil; Village Doctor; Teddy the Tiler; John Jones*

1840
26 Feb DL *Mountain Sylph; Raising the Wind*
28 Feb CG *Love; Patter v Clatter*
3 Mar CG *Legend of Florence; He Would Be An Actor; Fairest Isle*
6 Mar CG *School for Scandal; Harlequin & the Merry Devil of Edmonton*
10 Mar CG *Legend of Florence; Champs Elysées; Beggar's Opera*
14 Mar HM *Sonnambula; The Gipsy*
17 Mar Hay *The Rivals; His Last Legs; Tom Noddy's Secret*
18 Mar CG *The Rivals*
24 Mar CG *The Wonder; Champs Elysées*
26 Mar CG *Romeo & Juliet; One Hour*
28 Mar HM *Beatrice di Tenda; La Tarantella*
4 Apr HM *Sonnambula; La Tarantella*
7 Apr CG *Much Ado About Nothing; Twice Killed*
10 Apr CG *Hamlet; Ring Doves*
11 Apr HM *Lucia di Lammermoor; Cachucha & Tarantella*
25 Apr HM *Puritani*

1 May St J. *Don Giovanni*
5 May HM *Otello*
7 May CG *Sleeping Beauty*
9 May HM *Gazza Ladra*
12 May HM *Otello*
15 May CG *Twelfth Night; Sleeping Beauty*
16 May HM *Lucia di Lammermoor; Lac des Fées*
19 May HM *Gazza Ladra*
21 May HM *Don Giovanni*
26 May HM *Don Giovanni; Lac des Fées*
30 May HM *Inez de Castro*
9 June HM *Barber of Seville*
13 June HM *Barber of Seville*
20 June HM *L'Elisir; L'Ombre*
23 June HM *Lucrezia Borgia; L'Ombre*
24 June St J. *Jessandra*
27 June HM *Il Guiramento*
7 July HM *L'Elisir*
10 July St J. *Freischütz*
11 July HM *Matrimonio Segretto*
17 July St J. *Iphegenie en Tauride*
18 July HM *L'Elisir*
21 July HM *Anna Bolena*
25 July HM *Lucia di Lammermoor*
28 July HM *Lucrezia Borgia*
1 Aug HM *La Dama del Lago*
4 Aug HM *La Dama del Lago*

1841
5 Feb CG *Midsummer Night's Dream; Castle of Otranto* or *Harlequin & the Giant Helmet*
26 Feb Hay *Money; King's Barber; John Jones*
6 Mar CG *London Assurance; Captain of the Watch*
13 Mar HM *Orazi & Curiazi; Diable Amoureux*
17 Mar HM *Orazi & Curiazi*
19 Mar DL *Fidelio*
20 Mar HM *Tancredi*
24 Mar DL *Masaniello*
27 Mar HM *Tancredi; Diable Amoureux*
30 Mar CG *Keolanthe*
31 Mar DL *Tito*
22 Apr HM *Puritani*
24 Apr HM *Norma*
27 Apr HM *Puritani*
29 Apr HM *Otello*
8 May HM *Matrimoni Segretto*
15 May HM *La Straniera*
18 May HM *Norma; Lac des Fées*
25 May HM *Don Giovanni*
29 May HM *Fausta*

1 June HM *Fausta; Lac des Fées*
4 June HM *Horace*
5 June HM *Lucia; Lac des Fées*
11 June DL *Magic Flute*
12 June HM *Semiramis*
18 June DL *Robert le Diable*
19 June HM *Lucrezia Borgia*
21 June HM *Marie Stuart*
22 June HM *Sonnambula; La Sylphide*
26 June HM *Matrimonio Segretto*
29 June HM *Roberto Devreux; La Gitana*
2 July HM *Bajazet*
3 July HM *Lucrezia Borgia; Pas de Trois*

1842
4 Feb CG *School for Scandal; Guy Earl of Warwick* or *Harlequin & Dun Cow*
9 Mar CG *Bubbles of the Day; Comus*
11 Mar DL *Gisippus; Poor Soldier*
15 Mar HM *Gemma di Vergi; Giselle*
18 Mar DL *Gisippus; Acis & Galatea*
4 Apr DL *Macbeth; Students of Rome*
5 Apr CG *Bubbles of the Day; The White Cat*
8 Apr Hay *The Stranger; Foreign Affairs; My Wife's Dentist*
16 Apr HM *L'Elisir; Giselle*
18 Apr Hay *Gamester; Pretty Girls of Stillberg; Spring & Autumn*
29 Apr CG *Marriage of Figaro; White Cat*
30 Apr HM *Torquato Tasso*
3 May HM *Lucia di Lammermoor*
4 May St J. *Misanthrope; Valérie; La Jeune Femme en Colère*
17 May HM *Lucrezia Borgia; L'Étude d'Amour*
28 May HM *La Cantatrice Villaine; L'Étude d'Amour*
31 May HM *Elena di Feltre*
13 June St J. *Les Vieux Péchés; La Gamin de Paris; L'Ange au 6me. Étage*
27 June CG *Les Huguenots*
28 June HM *Puritani; Alma*
1 July CG *Les Huguenots*

1843
27 Feb St J. *Meunère de Marly; La Dame de l'Empire*
28 Feb CG *Donna del Lago; Miller & His Men*
13 Mar CG *Oberon; The Maid of Cashmere*
27 Mar St J. *Clémence*
1 June HM *Linda di Chamonix*
12 June DL *As You Like It; A Thumping Legacy*

13 June HM *Barber of Seville*
21 June St J. *L'Oncle Baptiste; Michel Perrin*
24 June CG *Ondine*
8 July HM *Don Pasquale; Ondine*
12 July St J. *Kempten ou Le Garrick Allemand*
20 July HM *Barber of Seville; Ballet*
22 July HM *Don Pasquale*
25 July HM *Norma*
29 July HM *Cenerentola*

1844
1 Feb DL *The Bohemian Girl; Harlequin & King Pepin*
2 Feb St J. *Stradella: Brasseur des Champs Elysées; Bruno le Fileur*
18 May HM *Zampa; La Gitane*
28 May HM *Matrimonio Segretto*
8 June HM *Barber of Seville*
18 June HM *Lucia; Le Délice d'un Peintre*
20 June HM *Don Carlos*
6 July HM *Lucia di Lammermoor*
11 Nov DL *The Syren; The Beauty of Ghent*
27 Dec DL *St Mark's Eve; Puck's Pantomime*

1845
4 Feb Hay *Old Heads & Young Hearts; Graciosa & Percinet*
6 Feb St J. *Catherine du La Croix d'Or; Chevalier de Gent*
22 Feb Hay *Somebody Else; Old Heads & Young Hearts*
24 Feb St J. *Don César de Bazan*
28 Feb Hay *The Sheriff of the County; Grandfather Whitehead*
3 Mar St J. *30 Ans dans la Vie d'un Joueur*
8 Mar DL *Robert le Diable; Giselle*
10 Mar St J. *Auberge des Adrets*
15 Mar HM *Ernani; Mazurka d'Extase*
3 Apr Hay *The Golden Fleece; Tom Noddy's Secret*
5 Apr HM *Sonnambula*
7 Apr DL *L'École des Vieillards; Le Coquin Imprévu*
19 Apr HM *Semiramide*
22 Apr HM *Sonnambula; L'Amour en Voyage*
24 Apr DL *William Tell; Clari the Maid of Milan*
26 Apr HM *Barber of Seville*
6 May HM *Ernani*
7 May St J. *La Tante Mal Gardée; Réné en Voyage; Robert le Diable*
8 May HM *Don Giovanni; Pas de Miroir*
17 May HM *Il Pirata*
20 May HM *Don Giovanni*

26 May Hay *Time Works Wonders; Monsieur Mallet*
30 May St J. *Les Fausses Confidences; Le Mari à la Campagne*
31 May HM *Don Pasquale*
3 June HM *La Pirata*
7 June HM *Lucia di Lammermoor*
17 June HM *Sonnambula; Esmeralda*
28 June HM *Robert le Diable*
1 July HM *Il Giornamento*
4 July DL *Les Huguenots*
8 July HM *Puritani; Esmeralda*
9 July DL *Le Postillion de Longjumeau; La Part du Diable*
11 July St J. *Le Poltran; Un Bal au Grande Mode*
17 July HM *Cosi fan Tutte; Pas des Quatres*

1846
23 Jan St J. *Un Secret; Tiridata*
26 Jan DL *Maritana; Harlequin Gulliver*
5 Feb Hay *Cricket on the Hearth; The Old School*
9 Feb St J. *Elle est folle*
19 Feb Hay *Orange Tree & Bee; Lend Me 5/-*
23 Feb St J. *Les Mémoires du Diable*
16 Mar St J. *L'Image; Péché & Pénitence*
20 Mar St J. *Femmes de 40 Ans; La Grisette; L'Héritière*
24 Mar Astley's
27 Mar St J. *Le Diable; L'Inconnue*
21 Apr HM *Sonnambula*
24 Apr St J. *La Demoiselle à Marier; Le Capitaine de Roquefenètre; Jean ou le Mauvais Sujet*
28 Apr HM *Norma*
1 May St J. *Jean ou le Mauvais Sujet; Le Père et le Fils*
11 May St J. *Jeanne & Jeanneta*
18 May St J. *Le Marquis de Rantzau; La Mère de Famille*
8 July St J. *Le Conte des Fées; Les Ethiopéans*
22 July St J. *Phèdre*
28 July HM *L'Ajo in Incharozzo*
4 Aug DL *La Favorita*

1847
18 Jan St J. *La Dame de St Tropez*
19 Jan Hay *London Assurance*
12 Feb St J. *Le Docteur Noir*
25 Feb HM *La Favorita; Coralie*
26 Feb St J. *Matilde; Les Deux Brigadiers*
1 Mar St J. *Le Petit Démon de la Nuit*
17 Mar St J. *Prince le Rouge*

19 Mar DL *The Bondman*
22 Mar St J. *Le Mariage au Tambour*
27 Mar HM *Ernani*
12 Apr St J. *Geneviève; Un Changement de Main*
13 Apr HM *Due Foscari*
16 Apr St J. *La Protégée sans le Savoir*
17 Apr CG *Semiramide*
19 Apr St J. *La Protégée sans le Savoir*
22 Apr HM *L'Elisir*
24 Apr CG *L'Italiana in Algieri*
30 Apr St J. *La Protégée sans le Savoir*
1 May CG *Puritani*
4 May HM *Robert le Diable*
6 May HM *Robert le Diable*
11 May CG *Semiramide*
12 May St J. *Le Mari à la Campagne; Médecin Malgré Lui*
13 May St J. *Ernani; Faint Heart Never Won Fair Lady*
13 May HM *Sonnambula*
15 May HM *Sonnambula*
18 May CG *Lucrezia Borgia*
20 May HM *Robert le Diable*
25 May HM *Sonnambula*
27 May HM *Fille du Régiment*
4 June St J. *Fourberies de Scapin*
5 June HM *Fille du Régiment*
8 June HM *Sonnambula*
10 June HM *Robert le Diable*
12 June CG *Norma*
15 June HM *Norma*
18 June St J. *La Carotte d'Or; La Fille de l'Avare*
22 June HM *Norma*
26 June St J. *Le Gamin de Paris*
26 June CG *Lucrezia Borgia*
29 June HM *L'Elisir*
1 July HM *Fille du Régiment*
3 July HM *Sonnambula*
8 July HM *Robert le Diable*
10 July HM *Fille du Régiment*
12 July St J. *Tancredi*
13 July HM *Sonnambula*
22 July HM *I Masnadieri*
23 July St J. *Andromaque*

1848
26 Jan St J. *Antigone*
9 Feb Hay *The Wife's Secret; Dearest Sir*
12 Feb Lyc *Golden Branch; Box & Cox*
14 Feb St J. *Rose et Marguérite*
22 Feb HM *Ernani*
6 May CG *Cenerentola*

18 May HM *Fille du Régiment*
20 May HM *Linda di Chamonix*
17 June HM *Lucia di Lammermoor*
22 June HM *Robert le Diable*
29 June HM *Fille du Régiment*
1 July HM *L'Elisir*
3 July Hay *Money; The Wonder*
4 July CG *La Favorita*
10 July DL *Henry VIII; Jealous Wife*
11 July HM *Lucia di Lammermoor*
15 July HM *Marriage of Figaro*
17 July HM *Fille du Régiment*
20 July CG *Les Huguenots*
15 Aug HM *Puritani*
28 Dec Windsor *Merchant of Venice*

1849
4 Jan Windsor *Used Up; Cox & Box*
11 Jan Windsor *Hamlet*
18 Jan Windsor *The Stranger; Twice Killed*
25 Jan Windsor *The Housekeeper; Sweethearts & Wives*
12 Feb St J. *Zanetta*
14 Feb Lyc *King of the Peacocks; An Appeal to the Public*
19 Feb St J. *Le Domino Noir*
23 Feb Hay *Merchant of Venice; Camaralzaman*
24 Feb DL *Franconi's Circus*
28 Feb St J. *L'Ambassadrice*
19 Mar St J. *Actaeon; La Double Échelle*
23 Mar Hay *Othello*
24 Mar CG *Masaniello*
27 Mar CG *Masaniello*
30 Mar St J. *Les Diamants de la Couronne*
31 Mar Lyc *Court Beauties; Hold Your Tongue; A Romantic Idea*
20 Apr St J. *Fra Diavolo*
21 Apr HM *Norma; Electra*
23 Apr Hay *The Sphinx; A Rough Diamond*
25 Apr Lyc *7 Champions of Christendom*
26 Apr HM *Sonnambula*
28 Apr HM *Lucia di Lammermoor*
1 May CG *Lucrezia Borgia*
2 May St J. *Le Pré aux Clercs*
3 May HM *Fille du Régiment*
5 May HM *Sonnambula*
8 May HM *Lucia di Lammermoor*
10 May HM *Robert le Diable*
12 May CG *Robert le Diable*
14 May DL *Freischütz*
15 May HM *Barber of Seville; Electra*
18 May St J. *Le Pré aux Clercs*
21 May DL *Stradella*

30 May St J. *La Part du Diable*
31 May HM *Don Giovanni*
2 June CG *Huguenots*
9 June CG *Huguenots*
11 June St J. *Domino Noir*
12 June Hay *Macbeth*
15 June DL *Martha*
18 June St J. *Ne touchez pas à la Reine*
20 June St J. *Comte Ory*
21 June HM *Lucrezia Borgia*
26 June Hay *Strathmore*
28 June CG *Huguenots*
30 June CG *Huguenots*

1850
1 Feb Windsor *Julius Caesar*
8 Feb Windsor *King Rene's Daughter;*
   Charles XII
13 Feb DL *Harlequin & Good Queen Bess*
14 Feb Hay *The Leap Year; The Serious*
   Family
16 Feb DL *Harlequin & Good Queen Bess*
18 Feb St J. *Le Chalet*
21 Feb Lyc *Island of Jewels*
25 Feb Hay *As You Like It*
27 Feb St J. *Le Val d'Andorre*
6 Mar St J. *Les Diamants de la Couronne*
8 Mar Hay *Hamlet; Royal Diamond*
11 Mar Hay *Much Ado About Nothing*
13 Mar St J. *Le Maçon*
16 Mar CG *Freischütz*
19 Mar HM *Nino; Les Metamorphoses*
23 Mar CG *Freischütz*
9 Apr HM *Barber of Seville*
11 Apr CG *Norma*
16 Apr HM *Don Pasquale*
19 June St J. *Catherine ou la Croix d'Or; Une*
   Caprice
25 June CG *Le Prophète*
27 June CG *Le Prophète*
29 June CG *Huguenots*
12 Dec Windsor *Henry IV: 1*
19 Dec Windsor *The Critic; The Practical*
   Man

1851
24 Jan Windsor *Prisoner of War; Loan of a*
   Lover
31 Jan Windsor *As You Like It*
3 Feb Hay *King Lear*
13 Feb Lyc *King Charming*
15 Feb Pcess *The Templar; Alonso the Brave*
   & the Fair Imogen

18 Feb Hay *Presented at Court; Good for*
   Nothing
20 Feb Pcess *Twelfth Night*
26 Mar Pcess *Love in a Maze*
28 Mar DL *Azrael ou Le Prodigal*
31 Mar Pcess *Pauline*
1 Apr HM *Gustave*
4 Apr Hay *Don César de Bazan*
8 Apr CG *Masaniello*
11 Apr Pcess *Love in a Maze; Pauline*
12 Apr HM *Masaniello*
1 May CG *Huguenots*
2 May St J. *Bataille des Dames*
3 May HM *Fille du Régiment*
6 May CG *Robert le Diable*
9 May St J. *La Camaraderie*
10 May HM *Le Tre Nozze*
13 May CG *La Donna del Lago*
15 May Pcess *Love in a Maze; Prisoner of*
   War
17 May CG *Freischütz*
20 May HM *Fidelio*
27 May CG *Fidelio*
29 May CG *Huguenots*
30 May St J. *La Dernière Coquette*
6 June St J. *Polyeucte*
7 June HM *Don Pasquale*
9 June St J. *Adrienne Lecouvreur*
10 June CG *Don Giovanni*
12 June HM *Le Prodigue*
14 June CG *Don Giovanni*
17 June HM *Le Prodigue*
21 June CG *Le Prophète*
1 July HM *Le Prodigue*
5 July HM *Florinda*
10 July CG *Magic Flute*
15 July CG *Magic Flute*
17 July HM *Le Prodigue*

1852
9 Jan Windsor *Twelfth Night*
16 Jan Windsor *Not a Bad Judge; The*
   Lottery Ticket
23 Jan Windsor *Legend of Florence*
30 Jan Windsor *The Jacobite; Swiss Cottage*
2 Feb Pcess *Billy Taylor; Merchant of Venice*
13 Feb Hay *A Duel in the Dark; Princess*
   Radiant
16 Feb Lyc *The Game of Speculation; The*
   Prince of Happy Land
18 Feb Pcess *King John*
21 Feb Pcess *The Iron Chest; To Parents &*
   Guardians

133

27 Feb St J. *Le Marquis de Lauzun; Roland Furieux; Lisette de Beranger*
28 Feb Pcess *Corsican Brothers; Swiss Cottage*
4 Mar Pcess *Corsican Brothers; Model of a Wife; Betsy Baker*
5 Mar Lyc *Game of Speculation*
22 Mar St J. *Ruy Blas*
23 Mar Pcess *Corsican Brothers; The Honeymoon*
26 Mar Pcess *King John; A Model of a Wife*
31 Mar Hay *White Magic; London Assurance*
2 Apr St J. *Paillasse*
3 Apr CG *William Tell*
19 Apr Pcess *Corsican Brothers; Wittikind & His Brothers*
20 Apr CG *Les Martyres*
21 Apr St J. *Mlle. de la Seiglière*
24 Apr HM *Norma*
26 Apr Pcess *Wittikind & His Brothers*
27 Apr Lyc *A Chain of Events*
30 Apr St J. *La Bataille de Dames; Marquis de Senneture*
1 May CG *Les Huguenots*
4 May HM *La Cenerentola*
6 May CG *Don Giovanni*
7 May St J. *Geneviève; Brutus, Lâche César*
8 May CG *Les Huguenots*
11 May CG *Magic Flute*
15 May Pcess *Lucky Friday; Corsican Brothers*
18 May CG *Magic Flute*
20 May CG *La Juive*
28 May St J. *Le Collier de Perles; Le Piano de Berthe*
29 May HM *Sonnambula; La Prova d'un Opera Seria*
31 May St J. *Yelva; Brutus. Lâche César*
2 June St J. *Egmont*
3 June CG *Les Huguenots*
5 June St J. *Don Carlos*
12 June St J. *Kabale & Liebe*
14 June Pcess *Vampire; Trial of Love*
15 June St J. *Margaretserbe*
17 June Hay *Keeley Worried by Buckstone; The Foundlings*
18 June Pcess *Corsican Brothers; The Trial of Love*
19 June CG *Robert le Diable*
21 June Pcess *King John; The Vampire*
22 June St J. *Faust*
24 June CG *Les Huguenots*
26 June St J. *Hamlet*
28 June St J. *Le Nuit aux Soufflets; Le Poisson d'Avril*

1853
7 Jan Windsor *Henry IV: 2*
14 Jan Windsor *Captain of the Watch; The Windmill*
21 Jan Windsor *St. Cupid*
28 Jan Windsor *Paul Pry; A Lucky Friday*
4 Feb Windsor *Macbeth*
15 Feb Pcess *St Cupid*
16 Feb Hay *Not So Bad As We Seem; To Paris & Back for £5*
18 Feb Pcess *Macbeth; Spitalfield Weavers*
21 Feb Lyc *Good Woman in the Wood*
24 Feb Hay *Masks & Faces; Not So Bad As We Seem*
25 Feb St J. *York; Le Chevalier de Dames*
2 Mar Pcess *Macbeth; Harlequin Cherry & Fair Star*
4 Mar St J. *Laure & Delphe*
8 Mar *King John*
10 Mar Pcess *Macbeth; Harlequin Cherry & Fair Star*
11 Mar Hay *The Serious Family; Masks & Faces*
14 Mar St J. *Une Petite Fille de la Grande Armée*
16 Mar St J. *Incertitudes de Rosette; Livre III, Chapitre I; Robert-Houdin*
2 Apr Pcess *Marco Spada*
4 Apr St J. *L'Image; Les Extrémes se Touchent*
20 May St J. *Mari à la Campagne; Bonhomme Jadis*
28 May St J. *Mlle de la Seiglière*
2 June CG *Les Huguenots*
4 June CG *Les Huguenots*
11 June St J. *Adrienne Lecouvreur*
14 June CG *Robert le Diable*
18 June Pcess *Sardanapalus*
21 June Hay *Mr Buckstone's Ascent of Mount Parnassus*
23 June CG *Lucrezia Borgia*
24 June St J. *Diane*
25 June CG *Benvenuto Cellini*
27 June St J. *Lady Tartuffe*
5 July CG *Le Prophète*
13 July DL *Wilhelm Tell*
15 July DL *Donna Diana*
6 Aug CG *Jessandra*
10 Nov Windsor *Henry V*
17 Nov Windsor *A Game of Speculation; Little Toddlekins*

1854
12 Jan Windsor *Money*

19 Jan Windsor *Honeymoon; Camp at Chobham*

26 Jan Windsor *Tender Precautions; Bengal Tiger*

2 Feb Windsor *Tempest*

14 Feb Pcess *The Lancers; Miller & His Men*

16 Feb Lyc *Once Upon a Time There Were Two Kings*

17 Feb Hay *Guy Mannering; Silver Hair & Three Bears*

23 Feb Lyc *Bachelor of Arts; Patter v Clatter*

24 Feb Pcess *Richard III*

28 Feb Hay *Ranelagh; Pretty Piece of Business*

3 Mar Pcess *Richard III*

7 Mar Hay *Hope of the Family*

9 Mar Lyc *A Nice Firm; A Charming Widow*

17 Mar Pcess *Richard III; Away with Melancholy*

21 Mar Olymp *To Oblige Benson; First Night*

23 Mar Pcess *Corsican Brothers*

28 Mar Olymp *Lottery Ticket; Plot & Passion*

30 Mar Pcess *Lancers*

31 Mar Lyc *Nice Firm; No. 1 Round the Corner*

4 Apr Pcess *Married Unmarried*

6 Apr Olymp *Wrong Box; 1st Night*

8 Apr Olymp *Wrong Box; To Oblige Benson*

25 Apr Hay *London Assurance; Mr Buckstone's Voyage Round Leicester Square*

27 Apr CG *Otello*

29 Apr St J. *L'Abbé de l'Épée; La Partie de Picquet*

2 May Pcess *Faust & Marguerite*

4 May CG *Fidelio*

5 May St J. *La Grand 'Mere*

9 May CG *Barber of Seville*

10 May St J. *Sullivan; Le Mariage de Miroir*

13 May St J. *La Haine aux Femmes; Le Jeune Mari*

20 May St J. *La Pensionaire Mariée; L'Héritière*

30 May CG *Puritani*

31 May St J. *La Joie Fait Peur*

3 June St J. *Au Printemps; Le Mariage Forcé*

6 June CG *Barber of Seville*

8 June CG *Le Prophète*

10 June CG *Le Prophète*

17 June CG *Rigoletto*

19 June St J. *La Promise*

21 June St J. *Fille du Régiment*

22 June CG *Lucrezia Borgia*

24 June CG *Les Huguenots*

26 June Pcess *Courier of Lyons*

27 June CG *Les Huguenots*

29 June St J. *Fille du Régiment*

1 July Pcess *Courier of Lyons*

3 July St J. *La Sirène*

4 July Olymp *Happiest Days of My Life*

8 July St J. *Fille du Régiment*

11 July CG *Le Prophète; La Prova d'un Opera Seria*

13 July CG *La Favorita*

15 July St J. *Les Diamants de la Couronne*

12 Aug Hay *As Like as Two Peas;* Spanish Dancers

1855

16 Feb Pcess *Louis XI; Harlequin Blue Beard*

20 Feb Olymp *A Lucky Friday; The Yellow Dwarf*

22 Feb Hay *Romeo and Juliet*

27 Feb Hay Spanish Dancers; *The Balance of Comfort*

2 Mar Pcess *Harlequin Blue Beard*

6 Mar Olymp *Tit for Tat*

9 Mar Lyc *Take Away that Girl*

13 Mar Olymp *A Blighted Being; The Yellow Dwarf*

23 Mar Pcess *A Game of Romps; Away with Melancholy*

28 Mar Hay Spanish Dancers; *His Last Legs*

30 Mar Pcess *Louis XI*

19 Apr CG *Fidelio*

23 Apr Pcess *Muleteer of Toledo*

24 Apr CG *Le Comte Ory*

26 Apr Hay *New Haymarket Spring Meeting; Fra Diavolo*

28 Apr CG *Ernani*

3 May CG *Fidelio*

5 May CG *L'Elisir*

7 May Olymp *Tit for Tat*

11 May DL *Amateurs*

12 May CG *Trovatore*

15 May CG *Trovatore*

19 May CG *Puritani*

31 May CG *Don Giovanni*

2 June CG *Norma; Ena*

5 June Pcess *Henry VIII*

7 June CG *Les Huguenots*

9 June CG *Trovatore*

15 June Olymp *Still Waters Run Deep; Garrick Fever*

18 June Pcess *Henry VIII*

19 June CG *Trovatore*

26 June Olymp *Still Waters Run Deep*

5 July CG *Lucrezia Borgia*
21 Nov Windsor *The Rivals*

1856
10 Jan Windsor *A Wonderful Woman; Only a Half Penny*
17 Jan Windsor *The Jealous Wife*
24 Jan Windsor *Merchant of Venice*
28 Jan Windsor *Still Waters Run Deep; A Game of Romps*
30 Jan Hay *The Butterfly's Ball; She Stoops to Conquer*
12 Feb Olymp *The Discreet Princess*
14 Feb Pcess *Everyone Has His Fault; Harlequin, The Maid & the Magpie*
18 Feb Olymp *The Discreet Princess*
22 Feb Hay *The Little Treasure*
26 Feb Olymp *The Discreet Princess*
28 Feb Hay *Lend Me 5/-; The Beaux Stratagem*
5 Mar Hay *The Little Treasure*
7 Mar Pcess *Harlequin, The Maid & the Magpie*
11 Mar Olymp *Still Waters Run Deep; The Discreet Princess*
13 Mar Pcess *The First Painter*
14 Mar Hay *The Evil Genius; Spanish Dancers; Lend Me 5/-*
2 Apr Pcess *The Victor Vanquish'd; Charles XII*
3 Apr Hay *Spanish Dancers; Lend Me 5/-; The Evil Genius*
8 Apr Pcess *The Wonderful Woman; A Prince for an Hour*
10 Apr Olymp *Still Waters Run Deep; The Discreet Princess*
11 Apr Adelphi *Like & Unlike; Urgent Private Affairs*
15 Apr Lyc *Trovatore*
17 Apr Adelphi *Urgent Private Affairs; Mother and Child Doing Well*
26 Apr Lyc *L'Elisir*
28 Apr Pcess *Winter's Tale*
1 May Hay *Grimshaw, Bagshaw, and Bradshaw; Spanish Dancers*
2 May Pcess *Winter's Tale*
5 May Adelphi *Like & Unlike; Urgent Private Affairs*
9 May Hay *The Evil Genius*
26 May Olymp *Retribution; Stay at Home More*
31 May Lyc *Rigoletto*
3 June Pcess *Winter's Tale*

5 June Lyc *La Favorita*
7 June Hay *The Evil Genius; Spanish Dancers*
9 June Lyc *Medea*
14 June Lyc *Trovatore*
18 June Lyc *Maria Stuarda*
21 June Lyc *Trovatore*
27 June Lyc *Rosamunda*
3 July Lyc *Rigoletto*
9 July HM *I Capuletti ed I Monticchi*
11 July Pcess *Winter's Tale*
15 July Lyc *Puritani*

1857
15 Jan Windsor *School for Scandal*
22 Jan Windsor *Our Wife; Deaf as a Post*
28 Jan Windsor *Secret Service; Hush Money*
5 Feb Windsor *Richard II*
17 Feb Pcess *Midsummer Night's Dream*
19 Feb Adelphi *Barney the Baron; A Night at Notting Hill*
24 Feb Pcess *Aladdin; Corsican Brothers*
26 Feb Hay *Double-Faced People; A Wicked Wife*
27 Feb Adelphi *Barney the Baron; A Night at Notting Hill; In and Out of Place*
13 Mar Hay *A Wicked Wife; Lend Me 5/-*
16 Mar Pcess *Richard II*
18 Mar Adelphi *Barney the Baron; In and Out of Place*
20 Mar Pcess *Richard II*
24 Mar Hay *Life's Trial*
27 Mar Pcess *Richard II*
30 Mar Hay *Life's Trial; Double-Faced People*
6 June Lyc *Trovatore*
9 June St J. *Les Bouffes Parisiens*
13 June Pcess *Richard II*
24 June Pcess *Richard II*
25 June Lyc *Sonnambula*
27 June Lyc *La Favorita*
7 July Pcess *Tempest*

1858
19 Jan HM *Macbeth*
21 Jan HM *Rose of Castile; Boots at the Swan*
23 Jan HM *Sonnambula*
29 Jan Hay *The Rivals; The Spitalfields Weavers*
3 Feb Hay *The Rivals; The Sleeping Beauty*
4 Feb Pcess *Midsummer Night's Dream; The White Cat*
6 Feb Olymp *The Dogs of Duralto*
8 Feb Adelphi *Poor Strollers*
16 Feb HM *La Zingara*

25 Feb Hay *Much Ado About Nothing*
27 Feb Hay *Much Ado About Nothing*
23 Mar Hay *The Love Chase; Presented at Court*
25 Mar Olymp *You Can't Marry Your Grandmother; Ticklish Times; Boots at the Swan*
26 Mar Hay *The Hunchback*
12 Apr Adelphi *Poor Strollers; Caliph of Bagdad*
13 Apr HM *Les Huguenots*
15 Apr HM *Les Huguenots*
19 Apr Pcess *King Lear*
20 Apr Olymp *Ticklish Times; A Doubtful Victory*
26 Apr Pcess *King Lear*
27 Apr HM *Les Huguenots*
30 Apr Hay *Pluto & Proserpina*
1 May Olymp *Ticklish Times; A Doubtful Victory*
4 May HM *Trovatore*
8 May HM *Les Huguenots*
11 May HM *Don Giovanni*
14 May Alhambra '*Pantopticon*' *Circus*
17 May Adelphi *Janet Pride*
4 June Hay *An Unequal Match*
5 June CG *Barber of Seville*
10 June Pcess *King Lear*
13 June CG *Fra Diavolo*
19 June CG *Fra Diavolo*
24 June HM *Lucrezia Borgia*
26 June HM *Lucrezia Borgia; La Reine des Songes*
1 July CG *Martha*
3 July HM *Les Huguenots*

1859
2 Feb Hay *Undine*
15 Feb CG *Satanella; Little Red Riding Hood*
17 Feb Pcess *Macbeth; King of the Castle*
18 Feb Olymp *Mazeppa*
22 Feb CG *Satanella*
24 Feb Hay *An Unequal Match*
25 Feb CG *Satanella; Little Red Riding Hood*
28 Feb Olymp *Porter's Knot; Mazeppa*
1 Mar CG *Maritana*
4 Mar Hay *The Honeymoon*
6 Mar CG *Lurline*
8 Mar Olymp *Still Waters Run Deep; The Invisible Prince*
11 Mar CG *Crown Diamonds*
31 Mar Pcess *Henry V*
1 Apr Hay *London Assurance; The Critic*

4 Apr Adelphi *Masks & Faces; The House or the Home*
8 Apr Olymp *Porter's Knot*
12 Apr Pcess *Henry V*
15 Apr Hay *Everybody's Friend; Used Up*
9 May Pcess *Henry V*
10 May CG *Les Huguenots*
31 May CG *Martha*
3 June Adelphi *The House or The Home; Devil on 2 Sticks*
4 June CG *Norma*
7 June CG *Gazza Ladra*
10 June Olymp *Porter's Knot; Retained for the Defence*
21 June Hay *Used Up*
26 June CG *Norma*
30 June Pcess *Henry V*
3 July CG *Les Huguenots*
5 July CG *Les Huguenots*
7 July Hay *The Contested Election*
23 Nov Windsor *The Evil Genius; To Oblige Benson*
30 Nov Windsor *Romeo & Juliet*

1860
11 Jan Windsor *The Hunchback*
18 Jan Windsor *The House or the Home; One Touch of Nature*
31 Jan Windsor *Bachelor of Arts; 9 Points of the Law*
11 Feb Hay *Jealous Wife; Valentine's Day*
15 Feb Adelphi *One Touch of Nature; The House or the Home*
20 Feb Olymp *Alfred the Great*
21 Feb CG *Dinorah*
23 Feb Adelphi *Dead Heart*
24 Feb CG *Lurline*
28 Feb Hay *Overland Route*
1 Mar Olymp *Alfred the Great*
3 Mar Adelphi *Paper Wings*
6 Mar CG *Lurline*
7 Mar Lyc *Amateurs*
23 Mar Olymp *Uncle Zachary; B.B.*
26 Mar Hay *Overland Route*
27 Mar Adelphi *Still Waters Run Deep; Bengal Tiger*
30 Mar Olymp *Uncle Zachary; B.B.*
1 May Hay *Victims; Box & Cox*
3 May Hay *The Rifle & How to Use It; Pilgrim of Love*
5 May CG *Dinorah*
8 May Pcess *Fool's Revenge*
10 May CG *Fidelio*

15 May CG *Fra Diavolo*
17 May CG *Don Giovanni*
1 June CG *Orfeo & Eurydice*
8 June Opic *Uncle Zachary*
9 June CG *Fidelio*
12 June CG *Dinorah*
14 June Hay *Family Secret; Fitzsmythe of Fitzsmythe Hall*
16 June Olymp *Daddy Hardacre*
19 June CG *Martha*
23 June CG *Huguenots*
28 June CG *Norma*
30 June CG *Orfeo*
2 July Olymp *Merchant of Venice; Dearest Mama*
29 Nov Windsor *Daddy Hardacre; B.B.*
14 Dec Windsor *Babes in the Wood*

1861

17 Jan Windsor *Masks & Faces; My Wife's Mother*
24 Jan Windsor *Richelieu*
31 Jan Windsor *Contested Election*
5 Feb Adelphi *Colleen Bawn*
7 Feb St J. *Isle of St Tropez; Endymion*
8 Feb CG *Bianca; Blue Beard*
11 Feb Hay *The Rivals; Queen Ladybird & her Children*
14 Feb HM *Robin Hood; Tom Thumb*
19 Feb Adelphi *Colleen Bawn*
22 Feb Pcess *Don César de Bazan*
25 Feb CG *Domino Noir*
9 Mar HM *The Amber Witch*
11 Mar Opic *Chimney Corner*
14 Mar Adelphi *Colleen Bawn*

Command Performances, 1881–1901

Date	Company	Programme	Place
4 Oct 1881	Edgar Bruce	*The Colonel*	Abergeldie
1 Feb 1887	Mr & Mrs Kendal	*Sweethearts; Uncle's Will*	Osborne
26 Apr 1889	Henry Irving & Ellen Terry	*The Bells; Merchant of Venice* (trial scene)	Sandringham
6 Mar 1891	D'Oyly Carte	*The Gondoliers*	Windsor
17 Mar 1891	John Hare	*Pair of Spectacles; Quiet Rubber*	Windsor
4 Sep 1891	D'Oyly Carte 'C'	*The Mikado*	Balmoral
26 Nov 1891	Signor Lago	*Cavalleria Rusticana*	Windsor
8 Nov 1892	Carl Rosa	*Daughter of the Regiment*	Balmoral
3 Dec 1892	Covent Garden	*Carmen*	Windsor
18 Mar 1893	Irving & Terry	*Becket*	Windsor
27 June 1893	Comédie Française	*L'Eté de St Martin; La Joie Fait Peur*	Windsor
15 July 1893	Covent Garden	*L'Amico Fritz; Cavalleria Rusticana*	Windsor
26 Oct 1893	John Hare & Mr & Mrs Bancroft	*Diplomacy*	Balmoral
13 Nov 1893	Carl Rosa	*Fra Diavolo*	Balmoral
18 May 1894	Eleonora Duse	*La Locandiera*	Windsor
19 May 1894	Covent Garden	*Faust*	Windsor
6 July 1894	Covent Garden	*Philémon & Baucis; La Navarraise*	Windsor
25 Sep 1894	Beerbohm Tree	*The Red Lamp; The Ballad Monger*	Balmoral
26 Feb 1895	R.C.M.	*Le Roi l'a Dit*	Windsor
24 May 1895	Covent Garden	*Trovatore*	Windsor
16 July 1895	Covent Garden	*Carmen*	Windsor
16 Sep 1895	George Alexander	*Liberty Hall*	Balmoral
22 Apr 1897	Sarah Bernhardt	*Jean Marie*	Cimiez
27 June 1898	Covent Garden	*Roméo & Juliette*	Windsor
24 May 1899	Covent Garden	*Lohengrin*	Windsor
4 July 1899	Covent Garden	*Le Chalet; Pagliacci*	Windsor
26 June 1900	Covent Garden	*Cavalleria Rusticana; Carmen*	Windsor
16 July 1900	Covent Garden	*Faust*	Windsor

Index

139

Index

Index

Money, 40, 45, 54, 59
Monte Cristo, 45
The Mountain Sylph, 30
Mozart, Wolfgang Amadeus, 31, 37
Much Ado About Nothing, 59, 96

Nabucco (Nino), 34
Napoleon III, Emperor, 69
La Navarraise, 110
Norma, 12, 31, 32, 36
Not a Bad Judge, 63
Not So Bad As We Seem, 72

Oberon, 69
One Hour, or The Carnival Ball, 16
Old Vic Theatre, 26
Olympic Theatre, 16, 39, 59, 63, 76–8, 95, 96
Only a Halfpenny, 49
Osborne, 29, 65, 81, 85, 87, 88, 89, 115;
    family theatricals at, 85, 89, 91, 92;
    Kendals' performances at, 89, 92, 101, 103
Otello (Rossini), 13, 26, 33
Otello (Verdi), 35
Ours, 97
The Overland Route, 65
Oxenford, John, 17

Paganini, Niccoló, 12
Pagliacci, 111
A Pair of Spectacles, 102, 103–4, 113
Pantomimes, 24–5, 71, 75
Pasta, Giuditta, 12
Patience, 98, 107
Peile, F. Kinsey, 104
Persiani, Fanny, 13, 32, 33
Phèdre, 43
Phelps, Samuel, 29, 51, 53, 54, 59, 60, 61, 63, 64
Phillips, Watts, 78
Phipps, Colonel Charles Beaumont, 46, 47–8, 52, 60, 62, 63, 64
Pinero, Arthur Wing, 113
Pink Dominos, 113
Planché, James Robinson, 12, 75
Polyeucte, 43
Ponsonby, Arthur, 87
Ponsonby, Frederick ('Fritz'), 87, 88
Ponsonby, Sir Henry, 80, 87, 89, 94–5, 108, 115
Poor Pillicoddy, 88
Popping the Question, 88
The Porter's Knot, 78
The Prince of the Happy Land, 75

Prince of Wales's Theatre, 98, 99
Princess's Theatre, 34, 51, 52–3, 54, 56, 57, 58, 59, 60, 66, 71, 73, 95, 103
Probyn, Sir Dighton, 100
I Puritani, 13, 15, 31–2

A Quiet Rubber, 102
Quin, James, 74, 80

Rachel (Elisa Félix), 42–3, 45, 67, 68
Racine, Jean, 43, 81–3
Raising the Wind, 30
Ramsay, Lady Patricia ('Patsy'), 92
The Rape of the Lock, 17
Ravogli, Giulia, 109
Reade, Charles, 75
The Red Lamp, 102, 107
Red Riding Hood, 83
Reszke, Edouard de, 110
Reszke, Jean de, 110–11
Richard II, 49, 54, 56, 60
Richard III, 20, 21, 56
Richelieu, 22, 24, 54, 64
Rigoletto, 34, 70
Ristori, Adelaide, 67, 68, 77
The Rivals, 49, 54
Robert le Diable, 35, 36, 37
Robertson, Agnes, 79
Robertson, T. W., 54, 95, 97, 105, 113
Robson, E. M., 104
Robson, Frederick, 54, 63, 77–8, 95, 104
Romeo and Juliet, 54, 63, 74, 96
Rorke, Kate, 103
Rosamunda, 68
The Rose of Castile, 38, 61
Rossini, Gioacchino Antonio, 13, 25, 26, 31, 32–4
Rubini, Giovanni, 13, 32, 33, 66
Russell, Lord John and Lady, 35
Ruy Blas, 44

Sadler's Wells Theatre, 29, 62, 63, 64
St George and the Dragon, 24
St James's Theatre, 29, 35, 41–2, 52, 59, 67, 103–5, 114; as Théâtre Français, 42–5, 67, 105
St Mark's Eve, 38
Sandringham, Command Performances at, 100, 101, 103, 105–6
Sanger's Circus, 'Lord' George, 93
Satanella, 38
Savoy Theatre, 94, 95, 114
Schiller, Friedrich, 33, 64, 68
The School for Scandal, 51, 54, 69, 103